The Course Portfolio

How Faculty Can Examine Their Teaching to Advance Practice and Improve Student Learning

Pat Hutchings, Editor

A PUBLICATION
OF THE AMERICAN
ASSOCIATION FOR
HIGHER EDUCATION
WASHINGTON, DC

AAHE
AMERICAN ASSOCIATION
FOR HIGHER EDUCATION

The Course Portfolio: How Faculty Can Examine Their Teaching to Advance Practice and Improve Student Learning
Pat Hutchings, editor

For more about AAHE and The Carnegie Foundation for the Advancement of Teaching, see pp. 119-121. Additional copies of this publication are available from AAHE Publications. For ordering information, contact:

AMERICAN ASSOCIATION FOR HIGHER EDUCATION
One Dupont Circle, Suite 360
Washington, DC 20036-1110
(ph) 202/293-6440 x11, (fax) 202/293-0073, (email) pubs@aahe.org, (web) www.aahe.org

ISBN 1-56377-043-1

CONTENTS

Preface

Margaret A. Miller, President, American Association for Higher Education

We have a problem in the modern academy: When the time comes to distribute the prizes, much of the most important and useful work of faculty is invisible. Researchers who trace the evidence of particles too small to imagine are rewarded; those who trace the effects of deep learning, sometimes equally elusive, are without honor in their own country. Many faculty members are becoming increasingly dissatisfied with this state of affairs, wanting recognition for their experiments with emerging forms of teaching that seem to invoke deeper, longer-lasting student understanding. Meanwhile, those outside the campus whose support is critical to its well-being — students, parents, policymakers, and politicos — blame their increasing dissatisfaction with the student experience on the way faculty worklife is organized and rewarded.

Enter *Scholarship Reconsidered* (1990), which has been rightly invoked throughout this volume. In that exquisitely timed book, Ernest Boyer (working with the able assistance of AAHE's own R. Eugene Rice) first captured and codified *all* the kinds of scholarship in which academics might engage, and suggested that more than one of them, what Boyer called the "scholarship of discovery," should be supported and rewarded.

The scholarship of discovery has prevailed in academic life for many reasons, including that it entails public performance in a clearly defined genre, as Lee Shulman says in chapter 1. In the world of quantum physics, observation is a necessary condition of existence; in the professional world too, purely private activity vanishes like snow in spring. For the other forms of scholarship to be recognized, they too need to be publicly observed.

Since 1994, in an ambitious national project supported by the William and Flora Hewlett Foundation and the Pew Charitable Trusts, AAHE has been creating ways to treat teaching as a scholarly activity that can be shared, documented, studied, reviewed, rewarded, and continuously improved — and that leads to learning. That project, From Idea to Prototype: The Peer Review of Teaching, assembled faculty and administrators from 16 campuses to create the new genres for this form of scholarship. Not the only but perhaps the most promising one to emerge was the course portfolio. Its inventor, William Cerbin, a professor of psychology at the University of Wisconsin-La Crosse and another name you will see throughout this volume, describes the course portfolio as "like a scholarly manuscript," a kind of laboratory notebook for faculty research into student learning and how to generate it. In its containment and focus on a particular "experiment," it more closely resembles the products of the scholarship of discovery than does its fraternal twin, the teaching portfolio.

The course portfolio is appealing for other reasons, as well. First, it puts the focus not simply on teacher practice but on its effect, student learning. We continuously measure collegiate learning, but we generally do so for what it tells us about students. In the course portfolio, learning is adduced instead as evidence of the effectiveness of the "transactional relationship," as Daniel Bernstein calls it, between the teacher and learner.

Second, in creating course portfolios, faculty members are both reflecting on student learning and learning themselves. Deborah Langsam reports, in case study 5, a comment of one of her portfolio's readers that personal "development is a (primarily) inward process." My understanding of learning is that it oscillates between the inward and outward: An experience, often social, is reflected upon; the record of that reflection receives feedback, which leads to improvement. That combination of personal reflection and social feedback describes the course portfolio perfectly.

The learning that results from the creation of a course portfolio benefits the individual teacher and his or her students, present and future. I think I am not unusual in having taught the core courses in my repertoire year after year, honing and perfecting my approach over time. I am also not alone, I am sure, in applying the lessons I learned in one classroom to others. The creation of a course portfolio requires a kind of focus, clarity of intention, and attentiveness to results that can improve that process enormously.

But because the portfolio process and its results are public, they reach beyond the local environment. This is a key characteristic of scholarship — others can benefit from the lessons the scholar learns — and also how practical wisdom forms and is passed down in human communities. I envision a time when faculty headed toward emerithood will spend their last years in the classroom creating coherent records of their practice on which their younger colleagues can build, rather than leaving behind masses of teaching notes that no one ever tries to decipher.

The working out of new forms of scholarship, like all deep reform, requires the patience and persistence of a number of very thoughtful people. Pat Hutchings was formerly the director of AAHE's Teaching Initiatives and now, as senior scholar for the Carnegie Foundation for the Advancement of Teaching, is the director of a new joint project of AAHE and the Carnegie Foundation, entitled the Carnegie Teaching Academy. Among those who have begun to give concrete form to Boyer's abstraction, Pat has been the leader. Lee Shulman too has been a major intellectual force in this work, joining AAHE first in the Peer Review of Teaching project and now as our partner in the next phase of this work. The Pew Charitable Trusts and the William and Flora Hewlett Foundation deserve our thanks for supporting not only the peer review work but also this volume. Most of all, I would like to thank the faculty, from William Cerbin on, who took the risk of going public with their teaching — who were willing to step out of the classroom closet, more or less in dishabille, in order to create this emergent form of scholarship. It is their work we feature here, and to them higher education owes a very large debt of gratitude.

Acknowledgments

Funding to produce this volume was provided by the William and Flora Hewlett Foundation and the Pew Charitable Trusts, which jointly funded the AAHE project that spawned it, From Idea to Prototype: The Peer Review of Teaching.

Many individuals contributed to this volume. It would not, of course, exist were it not for the generous work of the faculty who participated in AAHE's Course Portfolio Working Group, including several whose work is not directly represented here but whose contributions to the group's thinking and productivity have been essential (and whose work is published in other places, including earlier AAHE publications). Special thanks are due as well to Lee Shulman, who provided intellectual leadership — and much good spirit — for the portfolio group, and whose essay rightly begins this volume. Lee's role as president of the Carnegie Foundation for the Advancement of Teaching is an essential ingredient in advancing the scholarship of teaching and learning, which the course portfolio is designed to foster.

Finally, I would like especially to thank Laurie Milford, project assistant for the Carnegie Teaching Academy, and Bry Pollack, director of publications at AAHE. Laurie did the hard work of copyediting most of the volume, and she did the bulk of the work on the annotated bibliography that concludes it. Bry's good counsel and creativity have been essential throughout the writing and production.

P.H.

Introduction

Pat Hutchings, Senior Scholar, The Carnegie Foundation for the Advancement of Teaching

One of the central questions facing all professions is how to generate, exchange, and build on knowledge in order to improve practice. This volume explores that question in the context of the faculty's professional role as educators, and higher education's core function of teaching and learning. Its thesis is that the course portfolio — a relatively new development on the educational landscape — can help faculty investigate and document what they know and do as teachers in ways that will contribute to more powerful student learning. Readers will find an account of the genesis and rationale for the course portfolio, the context in which it has emerged and begun to evolve, practical guidance for developing and using it, and, interspersed throughout the volume, case studies by nine faculty members who have themselves developed course portfolios and generously share their purposes, processes, frustrations, and successes.

As noted in Margaret Miller's preface, much of the work and many of the ideas reported in the pages that follow are the product of a four-year national project on the peer collaboration and review of teaching. From Idea to Prototype: The Peer Review of Teaching, as the project was called, was coordinated by AAHE in partnership with Lee Shulman, who was at the time professor of education at Stanford University, and is now president of the Carnegie Foundation for the Advancement of Teaching. From Idea to Prototype brought together faculty teams to invent and explore a range of strategies for making their pedagogical work available to one another — be it for individual improvement or institutional decision making. As it turned out, the course portfolio was one of the strategies that provoked most interest and one, therefore, that a dozen faculty undertook to explore in a more sustained way by constituting what became known as the AAHE Course Portfolio Working Group. This volume stems from the group's commitment to "go public" with their work in order to assist others seeking to develop or use course portfolios.

The volume begins with a chapter by Lee Shulman designed to set the conceptual stage for what follows by putting the emphasis not on portfolios themselves, not on documentation per se, but on significant questions one might in fact explore through investigations of course teaching and learning. The three he proposes are surely not the only possible questions, but they wonderfully illustrate the need for a scholarship of teaching and learning through which faculty can contribute to and learn from one another's practice as teachers. The second chapter, by me, then focuses on the course portfolio itself as a vehicle for undertaking and preserving that scholarship. Written from my vantage point as director of AAHE's Peer Review of Teaching project and a member of the AAHE Course Portfolio Working Group, it answers, I hope, the questions many readers will bring to this volume about the definition and distinguishing features of the course portfolio and the purposes it can serve.

In chapter 3, "Why Now?," author Mary Taylor Huber answers this question by looking at three broad trends that help to explain and shape the current interest in course portfolios. In particular, she looks at recent developments related to faculty roles and rewards, including the efforts that have been catalyzed by Ernest Boyer's *Scholarship Reconsidered* (1990) and by the follow-up volume *Scholarship Assessed* (1997), which Mary, a senior scholar at the Carnegie Foundation, coauthored with colleagues Charles Glassick and Gene Maeroff. Mary's chapter is an edited version of a paper she originally presented at the 1998 American Historical Association annual meeting in a session about course portfolios in that field.

Chapter 4 is the "how-to" chapter — my attempt to provide practical guidance to those seeking to develop a course portfolio, looking at the predictable questions about what to include and how to organize it, but also how long it takes and how technology might help. My goal is not to provide a recipe or formula but, drawing on the work of the AAHE Course Portfolio Working Group, to suggest steps in a process and options for undertaking those steps. Because the matter of assessing and documenting student learning is so central to portfolio design, however, it is only glanced at in chapter 4 so as to receive a fuller treatment in chapter 5. Its author, Daniel Bernstein, was a participant in the Peer Review of Teaching project who joined the Working Group expressly to assist with "the assessment question" — an area he has been exploring for some time. Drawing on recent developments in assessment, Dan offers practical suggestions for including evidence about student learning in the course portfolio.

Chapter 6 comes to the topic that is, after all, a kind of bottom line: If I take the time to develop a course portfolio, will anyone read it — and what will she or he make of it? The literature now contains a number of reports on the use of *teaching* portfolios, but course portfolios are a newer and different thing; experience with them is more limited. Chapter 6, then, is necessarily cautious in its conclusions. But experience in several settings (including a study of portfolio readers in Australia reported by Kathleen Quinlan) suggests that course portfolios might indeed be useful vehicles for peer collaboration and review of teaching.

Chapters 1 through 6 are, if you will, the *exposition*; their authors attempt to synthesize, draw conclusions (albeit often tentative ones), highlight overarching themes, identify emerging questions. . . . The balance of the volume is *exhibition and demonstration*, in the form of nine case studies by faculty members who have developed and used course portfolios. For reasons of space, we chose not to reproduce the contents of the actual portfolios; but many of the case studies contain excerpts from them, and most of the cases, I believe, succeed in conveying a quite concrete image of this emerging genre. That is our hope. I and the other case study authors have endeavored, too, to be candid throughout, describing both the benefits and limits of course portfolios, both where they served us well and where they disappointed us or drove us nuts.

In an early conception of this book, the case studies were to be clustered together as a sort of appendix. As their centrality to the volume's themes and issues became clearer, however, we struck on the idea of interspersing them with the six expository chapters described above. Indeed, we have clustered the case studies in ways that will, we hope, provide useful glosses on those six chapters. For instance, the cases that follow chapters 1 and 2 elaborate on themes about the scholarship of teaching and learning that Lee Shulman and I address there. The two cases that follow Dan Bernstein's chapter on the assessment of student learning explicitly address the options for collecting and organizing such evidence as a centerpiece of the portfolio. At the same time, it should be said that the cases can certainly be read in any order. The book is not meant to be a forced march through the concept and practice of course portfolios, but rather a resource to be consulted and used in a variety of ways.

One final point about the nine cases: Because they illustrate so well the larger points of this volume, they are often quoted inside the six chapters, sometimes as examples in text, sometimes as boxes in the margins. For purposes of clarity, we have identified the source of such quotations in the most straightforward way possible, usually with "this volume" followed by the pertinent internal page number. They are not included in the volume's collected list of works cited.

Which brings me to the final chapter, "Resources for Further Work," developed primarily by Laurie Milford. Drawing on materials generated and collected through the work of the AAHE Course Portfolio Working Group, Laurie provides an annotated set of resources (books, websites, and other materials) to help readers set their own direction for future work on the scholarship of teaching and learning. Of special interest might be her leads to sources of actual course portfolio examples, which, as noted above, we do not offer in this volume but are increasingly available in other places.

Indeed, this volume is and should be simply a beginning — or, more accurately, I suppose, a part of a work in progress that has and will have many contributors, many manifestations, and products. Its authors set out to provide concrete guidance and examples that can point the way for faculty and campuses thinking about using course portfolios. But our larger ambition has been to contribute to evolving ideas about how professionals in higher education can create a scholarly community around teaching and learning that will value and improve practice over time. As editor of the volume, I am pleased to have been part of that effort and grateful to my colleague authors for their hard work and their generous contributions.

Course Anatomy: The Dissection and Analysis of Knowledge Through Teaching

Lee S. Shulman, President, The Carnegie Foundation for the Advancement of Teaching

This volume is a contribution to the evolving scholarship of teaching. The course portfolio is a central element in the argument that teaching and scholarship are neither antithetical nor incompatible. Indeed, my argument is that every course is inherently an investigation, an experiment, a journey motivated by purpose and beset by uncertainty. A course, therefore, in its design, enactment, and analysis, is as much an act of inquiry and invention as any other activity more traditionally called "research" or the scholarship of discovery.

Before launching into a detailed account of how a course can become an occasion for investigation and therefore a contribution to the scholarship of teaching, I must unpack and discuss both key terms of that phrase, *scholarship* and *teaching*. I shall begin this chapter with that discussion, then proceed to an account of the variety of ways in which the investigation of a course can proceed.

Scholarship and Teaching

For an activity to be designated as scholarship, it should manifest at least three key characteristics: It should be *public*, susceptible to *critical review and evaluation*, and accessible for *exchange and use* by other members of one's scholarly community. We thus observe, with respect to all forms of scholarship, that they are acts of mind or spirit that have been made public in some manner, have been subjected to peer review by members of one's intellectual or professional community, and can be cited, refuted, built upon, and shared among members of that community. Scholarship properly communicated and critiqued serves as the building block for knowledge growth in a field.

These three characteristics are generally absent with respect to teaching. Teaching tends to be a private act (limited to a teacher and the particular students with whom the teaching is exchanged). Teaching is rarely evaluated by professional peers. And those who engage in innovative acts of teaching rarely build upon the work of others as they would in their more conventional scholarly work. When we portray those ways in which teaching can become scholarship through course portfolios, therefore, we seek approaches that render teaching public, critically evaluated, and useable by others in the community.

What then do we mean by "teaching"? Too often teaching is identified only as the active interactions between teacher and students in a classroom setting (or even a tutorial session). I would argue that teaching, like other forms of scholarship, is an extended process that unfolds over time. It embodies at least five elements: *vision, design, interactions, outcomes,* and *analysis.*

Teaching begins with a vision of the possible or an experience of the problematic. The teacher holds a general view of how instruction might be improved, and/or senses that current instruction is unacceptable or a problem in some fashion. Vision leads to planning, the careful design of an instructional program or activity. A course design is much like the proposal for a program of research. The design can take the form of a course syllabus, a course outline, or even an argument for the development of a course. Usually, the design will eventually take the form of a detailed sequence of teacher and student activities, including topics, readings, projects, assessments, exhibitions, competitions, or demonstrations. Design might also include the creation of course materials, such as slides, demonstrations, simulations, websites, laboratories, internships, and the like.

Once designed, teaching must be enacted. Like any other form of inquiry, the course does not end with its syllabus but must proceed to delivery, action, and interaction. The actual enactment of a course is equivalent to the processes of carrying out a piece of research that has been designed. It is often punctuated by unexpected and quite unpredictable developments. The enactment of teaching is complex and demanding. It demands technical skills such as lecturing, conducting discussions, engaging in Socratic questioning, monitoring individual or collaborative projects, assessing student learning both informally and formally, and making midcourse corrections as needed.

Like any other form of investigation, teaching has outcomes. The outcomes of teaching are acts and products of student learning. A course once designed and enacted must yield tangible outcomes, changes in students' skills, understanding, values, propensities, or sensibilities. An account of teaching without reference to learning is like a research report with no results. It lacks its most essential ingredient.

Finally, the extended act of teaching (now accompanied by learning) remains incomplete without analysis. Again, like a research report, we are not satisfied with the unexplicated report of results. We expect the investigator to propose a set of interpretations of the significance of the investigation relative to the vision that initiated the study. What does the work *mean?* How does it extend the community's understanding of important questions? How will we act differently in the future as a result of these experiences?

In sum, a scholarship of teaching will entail a public account of some or all of the full act of teaching — vision, design, enactment, outcomes, and analysis — in a manner susceptible to critical review by the teacher's professional peers, and amenable to productive employment in future work by members of that same community. The course portfolio is a particularly fruitful example of the scholarship of teaching. And it is to a careful explication of the variety of ways in which a course portfolio might be organized, and to what ends, that I now turn.

Course Portfolios

Conversations about teaching and course portfolios often begin with questions about what goes in them. Those are natural, maybe even inevitable questions from the point of view of a faculty member first thinking about developing a portfolio. But to my mind, the harder questions one faces in developing the kind of systematic documentation and analysis of a course that many of us are now calling a "course portfolio" are not about how many dividers you need in an accordion folder. The hard questions are about how to represent and report the scholarship of teaching — assuming we believe teaching is indeed a legitimate form of scholarship — so that it can become part of the community's intellectual property; so that it can inform other members of the community, engage them in deep and significant conversations, provide a basis for the formation of communities of scholars, and be evaluated in that community.

The question I would therefore like to explore is, *What can one ask about a course in order to understand the ways in which its creation and conduct constitute a coordinated act of scholarship?*

Inventing a Genre

Note, first, that we take for granted the answers to the above question when it comes to the scholarship of discovery. That is, we have invented, in all of our fields, forms of display and communication called articles, monographs, performances, artistic creations, designs, and the like. Each field has its traditions and conventions about the questions you ask and the forms you use to display the fruits of scholarship for the evaluation and use of one's intellectual community. In reading dissertations, monographs, or articles in the natural and social sciences, for example, we have come to expect statements of the research problem, reviews of the relevant literature, and designs for the research, in that order, in the opening sections of the work. The expectation that we will encounter such sections serves as a template for the reader, not to mention a rubric for the referee or critic. Yet these are inventions, not revelations. They are conventions of the disciplines that have evolved over time to ease the communication of scholarship and its critical use. We do not need to read the raw data of lab notebooks, interview protocols, or historians' index cards. Each field has achieved an economy of inquiry and communication that compresses and transforms the processes of investigation.

Note too that these conventions did not appear spontaneously. They evolved slowly and painfully, over time, and they helped shape the scholarly communities in which they evolved.

This process of inventing conventions for capturing and conveying knowledge is the process in which we're now engaged with regard to teaching. That's what the course portfolio (or whatever it ends up being called) is all about: It is an effort to invent a form of scholarly inquiry and communication through which we can represent and exchange the scholarship of teaching, thus rendering it community property. As one of the participants in AAHE's Peer Review of Teaching project observed, developing a course portfolio was, for him, like "trying to write a short story before the genre had been invented."

My argument here is that until we find ways of publicly displaying, examining, archiving, and referencing teaching as a form of scholarship and investigation, our pedagogical knowledge and know-how will never serve us as scholars in the ways our research does. The archival functions of research scaffold our frailties of memory, and we need something comparable for the scholarship of teaching.

Moreover, intellectual communities form around collections of text — or these days, probably hypertext. Communities are identified, that is, by their discourse; and it is in large part because faculty (and teachers at all levels) do not have a shared language, a "discourse community," that our practice is often so disconnected, so isolating. As I have observed elsewhere, the "community of scholars" is alive and well when we wear our hats as researchers and engage in the scholarship of discovery or of integration. But as teachers we experience pedagogical solitude, we are isolated and cut off from the other members of our professional teaching communities.

Investigations of the Course

So, what kinds of questions might be used to organize and give shape to the course portfolio? What questions can help form communities of conversation and practice? Not surprisingly, the answer depends on the purposes for which a course portfolio has been designed, and the audience of colleagues intended to review it. But I would propose four different formats and themes that might be useful frameworks for our course investigations and documentation: the course as *anatomical structure*; the *natural history* of a course; the *ecology* of courses; and courses as *investigations*. The first three correspond to three standard types of question that biologists ask about an organism: What are its parts, how do they form coherent structures, and how do they function to support adaptation and equilibrium? How does the organism develop over time, and how does it adapt to changes and unexpected factors over time? How does the organism fit into the larger contexts of which it is a part?

Course Anatomy

One kind of question you might ask derives from the anatomical or biological metaphor. Courses, like organisms, comprise a variety of parts and structures, each associated with particular functions; one thinks of tests, lectures, discussions, internships, projects, laboratories. All these are elements of typical courses; they are the parts that are intended to cumulate into a well-functioning, adaptive experience. And, as in a structure-function approach in physiology, we can ask how these individual structures begin to interact and combine into systems. How well do the various parts fit together, amplify one another's properties, and aggregate into an effective experience of learning? How well do the systems work? This, then, is a route into the anatomy of the course.

This is a useful route, I think, because in good courses the parts mesh beautifully into a clear, well-articulated set of experiences. Students sense that what they are reading, practicing, investigating, and having evaluated cohere into a meaningful structure. The readings frame the labs, the quizzes both test and review understanding, large projects provide opportunities for integration and elaboration. In a well-crafted and well-conducted course, students experience an aesthetic sense of wholeness and coherence.

Conversely, courses that are unsuccessful are often those in which the pieces fail to add up. The goals of the course are incompatible with the assessments used to evaluate the quality of what is learned; the creativity of the exercises and experiences is a mismatch with the material covered in lectures. Such mismatches undermine the value that students place in all the components of the course and in the overall experience it entails. Moreover, it is likely that these discontinuities inhibit student understanding and motivation.

Natural History or Evolution

A second framework for a course portfolio is developmental or historical. We can, that is, ask about the way the course unfolds. What is its plot? What is its itinerary? What does it look like as narrative or as a journey? Does it have a denouement, or does it just end with a dull thud? What kind of "course" does the course follow, and how effective is the course in tracking the thematic purposes of the teaching and the learning? It is worth remembering here that the first definition of *course* (in my third edition of *The American Heritage Dictionary*) is "onward movement in a particular direction"; and that *curriculum* (the term we Americans use for a program of courses) comes from the Latin *currere*, meaning "to run," the same root one finds for *current*.

The point here, as in the course anatomy framework, is to uncover a qualitative difference. Some courses read like a great short story, building up tension, creating problems, and then providing ways of trying to resolve these problems — though, as with most good pieces of fiction, not all of them get resolved. Other courses, however, resemble a low-budget tour of France, where "if this is Tuesday, it must be Chartres." Topics and themes come tumbling one after the other, with little sense of logical necessity, narrative rationale, or cumulative sequence. It seems likely that the course whose plot or dramaturgy is well-crafted will hold the attention of students more effectively and consolidate their learning more durably. Of course, the evidence of outcomes will be necessary to transform that conjecture into a warranted claim.

Another kind of unfolding over time occurs across multiple generations of the same course, rather than within any one particular offering. Thus, a portfolio can represent the *evolution* of the course as it adapts to the consequences of earlier experiences as well as to new situations. This form of course portfolio might also read like the report of a course investigation, discussed further below.

Course Ecology

A third possible framework for a course portfolio is ecological. If the first kind of portfolio examines the course cross-sectionally, and the second type takes a longitudinal or narrative view, the ecological perspective places an individual course within its programmatic or curricular context. The ecological examination of the course explores where it fits in the larger program, be it curriculum of the major or of the minor, or — what is perhaps more important for many of our areas — where it fits into the education of students who are neither majoring nor minoring in our areas but are taking the course as part of a liberal education. "Ecology" means looking at the individual course as part of a larger system of instruction and learning.

Gerald Graff and others have pointed out that academics do not often ask questions about how individual courses fit into a larger curricular context. Such questions run against the grain of our prevailing conceptions of faculty autonomy and academic freedom. Nevertheless, this perspective is crucial if we are to achieve any kind of instructional coherence at levels beyond that of the individual course. Rare indeed is the course that can accomplish profound educational outcomes without the help of other courses that precede and follow it. A most important rationale for employing full-time faculty rather than the growing use of part-timers lies in the claim that full-time faculty members create a coherent curricular context among their offerings. An ecological perspective is important, too, because it may help us get at ways to characterize the contribution of an individual faculty member's work to the larger aims of the department or program.

Course as Investigation

Finally, we can approach the course as an investigation. The notion here is that every time we design or redesign a course, we are engaged in an experiment. The design of the course is in this regard a kind of working hypothesis; we teach the course hoping that what we intend is in fact what will transpire — and knowing full well that it won't be. Note that this overturning of expectation is what experience is all about: Experience is what you have when what you expected doesn't happen. When what you expected *does* happen — you drive to the office in the morning without incident — you haven't had an experience, and that is mostly a blessing. Too many real experiences would be intolerable. But experience is a source of learning, to the extent that when one encounters discontinuities between expectation and reality, between intention and accomplishment, critical learning can take place. The course portfolio might usefully be seen as a vehicle for probing such discontinuities, extracting from them important experience-based learning for future practice.

Such a portfolio — the portfolio as investigation — would follow the model of a research paper, raising questions, testing outcomes against expectation, measuring achievement, and critically analyzing the course as one would any other experimental or clinical intervention. The portfolio might be presented as the report of an experiment. It might also take the form of a clinical or ethnographic case. This model of the course portfolio bears the closest resemblance to work in the scholarship of discovery. It allows us to ask what we now know that we didn't know before about the teaching of this area, and how we might redesign our teaching practice in the future.

The Course Portfolio as a Condition for Discovery

The four frameworks above will, I believe, be useful organizers for our investigations of our teaching and our courses. They certainly do not exhaust the possible formats for course portfolios. Moreover, they overlap, in the sense that we can present structural, developmental, evolutionary, and ecological portfolios as course investigations. But one issue arises quite apart from the argument for any particular framework. It is a familiar issue I confronted when, in 1995, I presented the report of Stanford University's Committee on the Evaluation and Improvement of Teaching, which I chaired, to the Academic Senate. One of my colleagues, a distinguished department chair in the sciences, and a personal friend, got up and said, "Lee, you know, this interest in investigating and documenting teaching is all well and good, and in some perfect universe it would be great to do all this stuff. But, you know, we've got research to do. It's bad enough that teaching already interrupts our research — now you want us to do research on our teaching. And this is just going to take too much time. It's going to interrupt the flow of the real work of the university."

I do not dismiss this objection, even by suggesting that it is limited to that small fraction of our postsecondary institutions that are research intensive. I would like to address the question by referring to the research of UCLA anthropologist Eleanor Ochs. I heard Ochs describe her ethnographic studies of an international physics research group whose members were divided between Los Angeles and a university in France. I was struck by her account of what happens to this research group when its members have to prepare a presentation for the annual meeting of their disciplinary society. These meetings are very important for communicating one's work to the community, and for establishing the priority and importance of one's findings. Moreover, methods and findings must be displayed with great economy and precision, for there is an ironclad 10-minute time limit on each presentation. The investigators must interrupt the flow of their research routines and ask, What have we really learned that is important enough to pack into the allotted 10 minutes? How can we most vividly and persuasively display this work to our peers? Why must we stop what we are doing to tell others our story?

I'm sure you will recognize yourselves in this account. All working scholars are familiar with the frustration of having to interrupt important work to write proposals or to craft reports for funding agents, site visitors, or presentation at an important professional meeting. Ochs documents how having to prepare a paper not only occludes the flow of this research group's discovery process; it also initiates a dramatically different level of analysis, reflection, critical examination, integration, and reinterpretation of the research that has been otherwise rolling along. Suddenly the investigators have to move their deliberations from the private to the public domain, from sheltered discourse to public discourse, from the hidden to the revealed. Their challenge is far greater than simply to figure out which slides to use and which transparencies to reproduce. The processes of the discovery mode give way to a more pedagogical perspective. They not only must understand what they have learned from their research. They must represent that understanding in ways that will make persuasive good sense to others. Researchers must now frame their questions in new ways, pose new challenges, and respond to new demands. The interruption of the workflow for these purposes creates a crucible in which making sense of the research gets tougher as it strives to become more meaningful.

I am a member of many visiting committees and advisory boards. I've long ago concluded that the justification for an advisory board or a visiting committee cannot rest on the wisdom of the advice we give. The value of the visiting committee is that it obligates the people being visited to prepare for the visit by stopping their work, stepping back, and asking what it all means and how best to teach what they know to others in their community. That interruption is critical. It leads to kinds of learning and reflection that would be unlikely to occur under "normal" conditions. I have concluded that at two levels the occlusion or interruption of the processes of discovery is beneficial to the quality of scholarly discovery and integration. Similarly, the interruptions of typical teaching experiences that are engendered by the need to create course portfolios can have comparable benefits.

First, when I have to ask myself what I know that is worth teaching, and how I can simplify, reorganize, integrate, and represent what I know in ways that can be understood by others, that process — like the process of the scholar preparing for a paper at a national meeting — will loop back to shape and improve the teaching process itself. And that is why faculty who develop course portfolios so often report that the process of investigation, selection, and reflection entailed in writing the portfolio caused them to change the way they teach — to be more self-conscious about purposes, more vigilant about data collection, more thoughtful in assessing what works.

Second, having to take our teaching from the private to the public sphere, having to think about how we are going to engage in it, but also how we will come to understand what we are doing as teachers in ways that will permit us to organize what we do, display and communicate and converse about it to our own community, will have the same kind of improving effect for teaching that its parallel has for the improvement of the scholarship of discovery. Occluding the flow of either research or teaching leads to more serious reflection and analysis. These are the conditions for effective learning from these experiences.

It is too early to tell whether the forms of course portfolio I propose in this essay, or those that are presented elsewhere in this volume, prefigure the genres of scholarly discourse about teaching that will characterize the coming generation's efforts in this area. We appear to be entering an era in which teaching in higher education will be taken more seriously. The scholarship of teaching appears to hold significant promise as a vehicle for fundamentally changing the ways in which college and university educators view the chances for reconnecting the scholarships of discovery and of integration with the pursuit of scholarly teaching. But our attempts certainly represent legitimate movements in this direction, worthwhile experiments in the documentation and analysis of teaching.

Defining Features and Significant Functions of the Course Portfolio

Pat Hutchings, Senior Scholar, The Carnegie Foundation for the Advancement of Teaching

Lee Shulman's opening chapter frames the themes of this volume broadly; he puts the emphasis not on portfolios themselves, not on documentation per se, but on the need — and responsibility — that educators, like other professionals, have to investigate, understand, contribute to, and build on the knowledge and practice of their field. This chapter turns to the course portfolio itself as a vehicle for meeting this need and responsibility, addressing some obvious questions readers are likely to have: What *is* a course portfolio? What are its distinctive advantages? How might it be useful to me, my colleagues, and my campus?

For starters, it should be said that course portfolios belong to a larger universe of portfolio use, which is, after all, not new. Professionals in fields such as architecture and photography have used portfolios for years to document and display their best work. In some educational contexts, such as the teaching of writing, *student* portfolios have long been part of the teaching and assessment repertoire. Over the last decade or so, faculty looking for better, more "full-bodied" ways of representing their pedagogical work have developed *teaching* portfolios. Indeed, many readers will come to the idea of the course portfolio through its cousin, the teaching portfolio, so it may be useful to begin by defining the former in reference to the latter . . . and to say at the outset that the course portfolio is not meant to replace the teaching portfolio, which is well-suited to a more comprehensive account of one's teaching practice as part of a longer career. Rather, the course portfolio can be seen as a subset of the teaching portfolio, designed to accomplish certain purposes more fully.

Defining Features of the Course Portfolio

So what is a course portfolio? The best answer to this question is contained in the case studies that are included throughout this volume, in which faculty members from the AAHE Course Portfolio Working Group report in detail on their portfolio, how it came to be, what shape it takes, and what difference it has made in their teaching practice. As is clear from these cases, there is no single, standard formula for defining the course portfolio. Nevertheless, it is now possible, out of recently emerging practice, to make a number of generalizations about its defining features and comparative advantages.

A Focus on the Course

In contrast to the typical teaching portfolio, in which the faculty member documents practice in a range of instructional contexts over time, the course portfolio focuses on the unfolding of a single course, from conception to results. The premise behind this design is not that the course should be the privileged con-

> *"The course portfolio is a relatively new genre that is being developed to enable teachers to discuss both the scholarly and the pedagogical dimensions of their teaching; it provides a reflective outlet for articulating the intentions and experiences involved with teaching particular courses at a given time in a person's career."*
>
> RANDY BASS (THIS VOLUME, 91)

text for examining teaching and learning. Indeed, as many educators point out, too much emphasis on the course can exacerbate the problem of disconnected, fragmentary learning "in boxes"; as Randy Bass points out in case study 9, it is the cumulation of experiences over multiple courses that leads to important forms of learning. But the course is, after all, the unit, "the package," in which most faculty think and talk about and conduct their teaching, and it is also the context in which content and process, curriculum and pedagogy, come together in a way that has some "travel," some portability: That is, I may or may not be interested in knowing about a colleague's teaching practice in general (which is what I am likely to find in a teaching portfolio), but I might very well be interested in her experience with a course that I myself sometimes teach, or that I rely on as a foundation for one of my own or attempt to build on.

Moreover, it is in many ways at the level of the course that teaching — which is to say, learning — rises or falls. Often when we talk about teaching effectiveness, we talk about snapshot-like moments — a powerful exchange in the final five minutes of Monday's class, a really lively small-group exercise. But, as Lee Shulman put it in a 1996 presentation to an AAHE conference audience, most teachers can be

> superbly Socratic once a month.... The real embarrassments of pedagogy are at the level of the course: the course that just doesn't quite hang together; the course where the students can't quite figure out how what you're doing this week relates to what you're doing next week, or why a major assignment is connected to the central themes of the course. The more holistic, coherent, integrated aspect of teaching is often where we fail. (Shulman et al. 1996)

Conversely, it is at the level of the course that one sees real teaching excellence. The course is a powerful unit of analysis for documenting teaching because it is within the course that knowledge of the field intersects with knowledge about particular students and their learning.

The power of focusing not on the teacher's practice in general but on the teaching and learning in a particular course — and, as Shulman urges in chapter 1, on the relationship of one course to other courses — is a distinctive advantage of the course portfolio.

A Spotlight on Student Learning

Most teaching portfolios contain samples of student work, but the "unit of analysis" is primarily the teacher; that is, the purpose of the portfolio is to give a picture of the individual's teaching effectiveness. In contrast, the course portfolio puts the spotlight on student learning as the organizing principle. Steve Dunbar, one of the first members of AAHE's Peer Review of Teaching project to develop a course portfolio, wrote (in an earlier publication based on that project), "My portfolio is based on seven goals I've identified for students in the course, and my efforts to see whether I can get students to achieve them.... I just want to know whether I'm getting through to the students" (1996, 57).

The heart of the course portfolio, its center of gravity, is evidence the teacher gathers about students' learning and development (through the use of classroom assessment techniques, interviews with students, peer review of student work, and other strategies described by faculty elsewhere in this volume). Moreover, the decision to develop a portfolio, and the process of putting it together, prompts more frequent and systematic "data points." In case study 2, Donna Martsolf notes,

> *The primary benefit for me was the focus on student learning. Weekly student reflections, solicited in order to fill out the portfolio with relevant evidence, have helped me to clarify, and therefore more immediately address and correct, student misconceptions. As a result, student learning has occurred much more quickly this semester than it has in previous semesters. I have evidence that students understand the importance of theoretical thinking in nursing and that this understanding occurred as early as week five for some students and by week eight for all of them. (28)*

Of course, this examination of student learning is also a reflection on the quality of the teacher's work. Indeed, the relationship between student learning and effective teaching — and how to think about making the case for teaching in terms of student learning — has been a central challenge for the AAHE Course Portfolio Working Group, so much so that chapter 5 is wholly dedicated to this question.

A Scholarly Investigation

A question often asked of a teaching portfolio is, Does the work included fairly represent the teacher's practice? In contrast, the course portfolio is not so much an account of what the teacher typically does as an account of what happens when he or she does something deliberately and explicitly *different*. It is not, that is, a report of what *is* but a purposeful experiment and investigation — a process, if you will, of scholarly inquiry into what *might* be.

This idea of the course portfolio as investigation has become increasingly salient in the work of the faculty members featured in this volume. But it is also a conception that appears in the work of an individual whom many faculty interested in the course portfolio see as its first practitioner, William Cerbin. A professor of psychology at the University of Wisconsin-La Crosse, Cerbin recounts the impetus of his 1992 pioneering foray into the course portfolio precisely around this idea of scholarly investigation and inquiry. It is worth quoting at length:

> *Ernest Boyer's* Scholarship Reconsidered *appeared, and I was very struck by his notion of the scholarship of teaching — and how that notion might take us beyond the old saw that teaching is based on scholarly acumen in one's field, brought to bear in the classroom. I wanted to explore what it was that's scholarly about the teaching I do.... I was familiar with teaching portfolios.... But thinking about teaching as scholarly inquiry began to lead me in the direction of something I had not seen anyone else doing: a portfolio that focused on the course rather than on all of one's teaching. Being a social scientist, I began to think of each course ... as a kind of laboratory — not as a truly controlled experiment, of course, but as a setting in which you start out with goals for student learning, then you adopt teaching practices that you think will accomplish these, and along the way*

you can watch and see if your practices are helping to accomplish your goals, collecting evidence about effects and impact.

In this sense, each course is a kind of discrete entity with a beginning and an end, fairly discrete goals you're trying to accomplish, and, typically, a body of content you're trying to deal with.

So the course portfolio was a natural way to go for me, one that followed from my ideas about teaching and learning. I'm not sure I saw this immediately, but one thing I now see is that the course portfolio is really like a scholarly manuscript — not a finished publication, but a manuscript, a draft, of ongoing inquiry. (1996, 52-53)

An Emerging Model of the Course Portfolio

Like Cerbin, many faculty have become aware of and attracted to the argument that teaching can be seen and undertaken as a scholarly activity. Not by accident, the model of the course portfolio that has gradually emerged from early practice follows and enacts this idea in that its structure is modeled on the analogy of a scholarly project. That is, a well-taught course, like any good scholarly project, can be characterized as having (at a minimum) three elements of *design*, *enactment* or *implementation*, and *results*, as follows:

1. The course begins with significant goals and intentions, which are embodied in its design and expressed in the syllabus and other documents (such as a proposal to a curriculum committee).

2. Those goals and intentions are enacted or carried out in appropriate ways as the course unfolds over the term.

3. And, as a result, certain outcomes emerge: students grasp (or do not) the key ideas/methods/values of the field that shaped the course design and enactment.

While each of the faculty members whose work is featured in this volume takes a slightly different twist on the design of the course portfolio, readers will see that each has more or less followed this three-part structure of design, implementation, and results. In addition, each deals with another topic that is essential to any scholarly project: the "so what" question, the question about the meaning and implications that follow from the investigation. The course portfolio is an occasion for sustained reflective commentary that deals not only with what students learn but also with what the teacher has learned that might contribute to the "community of practice" that he or she belongs to.

This emerging model of the course portfolio has the distinctive advantage of representing the intellectual integrity of teaching. By capturing and analyzing the relationship or congruence *among* design, implementation, and results, it gets at that "more holistic, coherent, integrated aspect of teaching" that Lee Shulman points to as essential.

"But more than anything else, a constant flow of reflective statements at the start of each section helps clarify for the reader the instructor's conception of the course. Why did I choose to give this particular assignment? Is there a reason why my tests are so long? Do the test results indicate that the students 'got' the material? Without these reflective statements . . . the portfolio becomes simply a dumping ground for every piece of paper generated during the semester, and the reader comes away without a true feeling for the course."

ELI PASSOW (THIS VOLUME, 71)

Meeting Real Needs

Shulman's opening chapter provides a conceptual rationale for the course portfolio, but it may be useful to note as well four practical functions and needs that the course portfolio can help meet in a rather immediate way.

First, course portfolios are *an aid to memory*. They provide an antidote to the condition that Shulman has dubbed "pedagogical amnesia." Courses, he says, "are a bit like the choruses of songs; you expect to sing them more than once" (Shulman et al. 1996, 2). Indeed, most of us have the hope and expectation that we will teach the course better the next time, having learned from the current experience. And toward that end, we're sure that we'll remember, next year at this point in the course, what worked and didn't in, say, the group reports on the Flannery O'Connor story, or the design project in mechanical engineering, or the exam question about the Federalist Papers. But, somehow, time passes, and the details slip away. Shulman continues,

> There are certain experiences — teaching is one, and people tell me that childbirth is another — in which certain automatic acts of repression immediately follow the experience, wiping out both the painful and sometimes the pleasurable aspects of the experience, but leaving one fresh to try it again. But if we want to learn from teaching, we can't afford the expenses of pedagogical amnesia. And so one purpose of the course portfolio is to serve as a kind of aide de memoire. (2)

Indeed, for William Cutler, the course portfolio was not only an aid to memory but also, as he writes in case study 1, an aid to perception itself: "So many things occur simultaneously [in a college classroom] that no one person could ever notice, let alone account for them all" (19). Course portfolios encourage a kind of attentiveness, helping to create an archive where memory fails; they assist us as teachers to do that difficult thing: to learn from our own experience.

Second (harkening back to the three features of course portfolios described above), the course portfolio is *an occasion to investigate student learning*. Are my students learning what I think I'm teaching? Are they getting it? Or, to put the question in a more open-ended, investigative way: What *are* they learning? What *sense* are they making of the ideas we attempt to engage them with? What happens to their understanding of the field itself and of themselves as learners of it?

Of course, faculty have always had ways of assessing and keeping track of student learning: papers, projects, exams. But what most have not had is an ongoing habit of and occasion for investigating the student learning experience in depth and over time, looking not only at a column of marks in the grade book but also at messy, important questions . . . for Donna Martsolf, the question of how students progress toward a more abstract concept of nursing and nursing theory . . . for Randy Bass, questions about how hypertext forms of reading and writing can usefully complicate students' understandings of the nature of narrative. The course portfolio is a powerful occasion and prompt for asking important questions about student understandings.

Third, course portfolios are an *escape route from the isolation of the classroom*. Much has been said and written about this isolation. Jane Tompkins wryly likens teaching to sex in this regard: "Teaching, like sex, is something you do

"I was most interested in making my case to my own colleagues at Kent State University, but I also saw the portfolio as a vehicle for explaining my still fairly unorthodox approach to the teaching of nursing theory to colleagues at the national level. It was my chance to contribute to the scholarship of teaching and learning within the professional community."

DONNA MARTSOLF
(THIS VOLUME, 27)

alone, although you're always with another person/other people when you do it; . . . and people rarely talk about what the experience is really like for them, partly because, in whatever subculture it is I belong to, there's no vocabulary for articulating the experience and no institutionalized format for doing so" (1990, 656). Lee Shulman (1993) calls the problem "pedagogical solitude."

The good news is that solutions to the problem have begun to emerge: AAHE's *Making Teaching Community Property* (1996) includes reports by faculty about nine strategies designed to make the work that we do as teachers available to one another for discussion, improvement-oriented feedback, and formal review. One of these nine is the course portfolio, which attracted virtually all members of the AAHE Course Portfolio Working Group in large part because of its power to bring us into substantive conversation with others about our work. Such exchange is a matter not simply of meeting a need for a sense of connection and community but of providing a route through which teachers can contribute to and build on the work of others.

Finally, the course portfolio is a way of *bringing recognition and reward to teaching excellence.* As Mary Huber indicates in chapter 3, there is widespread interest in this goal on campuses and in the scholarly societies. The problem is that in many settings the evidence about teaching effectiveness is too paltry, too incomplete, to warrant such recognition and reward. The course portfolio is a step toward richer, more authentic, "situated" portrayals of what teachers know and can do, a significant advance on prevailing practice, which depends almost exclusively on student ratings. These ratings are important but, as Keig and Waggoner (1994) point out, limited: "[W]hen faculty and administrators allow student ratings to be the only real source of information about teaching, they unwittingly contribute to a system in which too much emphasis is placed on evaluating superficial teaching skills and not enough is placed on more substantive matters" (1). The aim of portfolios is not, it should be said, to replace student voices but to supplement, complement, round out the picture.

In conclusion, course portfolios are relevant to a number of real needs felt by real educators in their daily practice. They are not a panacea. They are not all figured out or failsafe or without a downside. But they *are* a step in the direction of a scholarly approach to teaching that can profoundly improve our students' learning *and* our own practice in fostering that learning.

Peer Collaboration and Review of Teaching Takes Many Forms

- Teaching circles
- Reciprocal classroom visits and observations
- Mentoring and coaching
- Focus on student learning
- Teaching portfolios and course portfolios
- Team teaching and teaching teams
- Collaborative inquiry and pedagogical scholarship
- Departmental occasions for collaboration, including hiring
- Intercampus collaboration and external peer review

(Hutchings 1996)

Writing a Course Portfolio for an Introductory Survey Course in American History[1]

William W. Cutler III, History, Temple University

The following case study describes and analyzes a course portfolio for History 67, The Economic, Social, and Political History of the United States to 1877, an undergraduate class in early American history at Temple University. I compiled this portfolio (to which I shall refer hereafter as CPH67) during the 1996-97 academic year, when I taught History 67 twice, once in the fall at Temple's suburban campus in Ambler, Pennsylvania, and again in the spring at the university's main campus in North Philadelphia.

An introductory survey course that is part of the university's core curriculum, History 67 covers a broad span of time, beginning with the precolonial era in North America before 1600, continuing with the colonial and antebellum periods in the United States from 1607 to 1861, and concluding with a short consideration of the American Civil War and its aftermath, Reconstruction.

The Idea of the Course Portfolio

CPH67 was not my first attempt at writing a course portfolio. During the spring semester 1996, I wrote one for a graduate course in the history and sociology of American education that I have taught many times over the past decade. This trial run taught me

just how difficult it is to document what transpires in a college classroom. So many things occur simultaneously that no one person could ever notice, let alone account for them all. Moreover, instructors never know exactly what students are thinking on any given day or how much they are learning. Traditional assessment tools in history such as quizzes and examinations are at best a reflection of actual instruction.

Though it is inevitably incomplete, being in effect the instructor's account of what went on, a course portfolio gives a fuller picture. Nevertheless, if we are to arrive at a better understanding of what teachers are trying to achieve and how well they achieve it, then it makes sense to put course portfolios together, no matter how incomplete or subjective such documents might be. Portfolio writers, on the other hand, have an obligation to flesh out their account with hard evidence, drawn from such sources as syllabi, examinations, readings, handouts, and samples of student work.

Uncovering the Scholarship in Teaching History

I prepared CPH67 to test the hypothesis that it could illustrate the ways in which a historian deals with an intel-

[1] *An earlier version of this essay was delivered as a conference paper at the 112th Annual Meeting of the American Historical Association, Seattle, Washington, January 11, 1998.*

lectual problem in the classroom. I developed this rationale during conversations with Dr. Noralee Frankel, the American Historical Association's assistant director for teaching.

She and I agreed that our colleagues in the discipline would never warm to the idea of course portfolios unless it could be shown that they reflect scholarship by demonstrating a historian's knowledge, imagination, and understanding. Designing and delivering almost any history course requires a teacher to possess all of these qualities. Given the vastness and ambiguity of the past, deciding what to include and how to present it surely represents a daunting intellectual problem.[2]

Organizing the Evidence

CPH67 is a large document. It amounts to nearly 300 pages, including appendices. I compiled most of it during the fall semester 1996, when I wrote the course narrative that informs the reader about the content that I taught that term, the pedagogical methods that I used, and the general rhythms of my instruction. Organized by week, the course narrative features a discussion of the ways in which three themes — freedom, diversity, and migration — shaped my lectures, discussions, assignments, and examinations. For example, it says the following about week three, during which I emphasized freedom and diversity:

> On Monday I asked the students to interpret the geography of a 17th-century New England town for the lessons it might teach about the relationship between the individual and the

group in Puritan society. Using overheads to show the nucleated layout of an open field town (e.g., Sudbury and Andover, Mass.), I was able to elicit from the students the conclusion that by placing their houses so closely together, the Puritans discouraged individual freedom in favor of group conformity. . . . We then examined how and why the residents of nucleated towns dispersed over three or four generations, and we discussed the ramifications of this dispersal for the Puritan concept and practice of community.

As an illustration of the pedagogical methods I used and the rhythms of my teaching, the following excerpt from my course narrative might be instructive:

> During week five I employed three different types of teaching strategies. On Monday I gave a lecture that set the agenda for the week; on Wednesday I taught the class by the Socratic method, using the concept of sovereignty as my organizational framework; on Friday, Mr. Wilson [the TA] conducted a quick review before we broke into small groups to discuss the questions he prepared.

Partners in My Portfolio Project

My department gave me teaching assistants, one in each semester. They were Mr. Martin Wilson in the fall and Ms. Jennifer Coleman in the spring. Both are doctoral students who were working in History 67 for the first time,

---

[2]The same could be said, no doubt, for many other disciplines, especially in the humanities and social sciences, where the choice content and the sequence of instruction are by no means preordained.

but Mr. Wilson was a more experienced teacher, who had even taught another history course at Temple on his own. They graded papers, gave a lecture, and ran one of our two weekly discussion sections. I asked each TA to keep a pedagogical diary, and these reflective statements offer an interesting and informative complement to my narrative and perhaps some reassurance that my narrative is not just self-serving.

The diaries composed by my two TAs differ in many ways. Mr. Wilson focused on his efforts to teach the course themes in his weekly discussion section. Ms. Coleman used her diary to test her understanding of the information that I conveyed in my lectures, giving readers of my portfolio a way to judge whether or not I was being understood, at least by one receptive listener. Both used their diaries to reflect on the success or failure of different lessons and to air their own anxieties about teaching. For example, Mr. Wilson wrote the following about an early class devoted to defining the discipline of history:

> *Professor Cutler talked some about how memory can be seen as the first step in assembling history. My feeling is that the class had a hard time understanding the concept of collective memory. They, for the most part, retained their first concept of the difference between memory and history. I would have liked to get into a discussion of how memory and history are similar. I think that explaining how memory changes with changing circumstances in the present, as does history, would have provided an important clue to the students about the nature of interpretation.*

Responses From Readers

In the fall of 1997, I submitted my portfolio for merit review at Temple University, and the two members of my department who reviewed it said that it provided them with a welcome means by which to judge my teaching. One of the two said, in particular, that he liked my portfolio's emphasis on defining course objectives and themes. He added that my portfolio might serve an institutional purpose by acting as a model for graduate students and junior colleagues preparing to teach this course for the first time.

I also sent the portfolio (minus some of its appendices) to Professor John Inscoe, in the History Department at the University of Georgia, who used it as a prompt for a teaching circle. He and his colleagues also thought it could serve as a model. They were particularly impressed by the two TA diaries, not only because they reveal something about how my course differed from one semester to the next but also because these documents augmented my narrative, giving another perspective on my teaching.

The Course and Its Purposes

Much of the documentation that I included in CPH67 is meant to show how I try to help beginning students make sense of early American history by organizing their thinking around the three course themes. Too often undergraduates get lost in the study of history, overwhelmed and disoriented by the amount of information they encounter in lectures and readings. My syllabus, the handouts that my TAs prepared for the discussion sections, and the examinations that we wrote were intended to solve this problem by encouraging students to think in terms of these themes. The syllabus prompts them thematically by asking them a series of questions about freedom, diversity, and migration that are linked to the reading for that week.

For example, there are questions designed to help them grasp the changing meaning and importance of diversity by encouraging them to look for material pertaining to Native Americans, women, and blacks. Other questions direct them to passages that explain how ideology, technology, business, and government transformed the meaning of freedom in the United States over time. Still others encourage them to find out about migration by reflecting on the textbook's or the supplementary reader's treatment of such topics as the Great Awakening, the Middle Passage, Manifest Destiny, and westward expansion.

During each semester, my students had to tackle these themes by writing 14 (fall) or 12 (spring) short essays about them based on the textbook and the reader. There are samples of these essays in the portfolio's appendix, representing the work of four students over time. Making students write about the assigned readings increases the probability that they will do it and remember something about it afterwards. Between the fall and spring semesters, I reduced the number of journal assignments, because in the fall many students had difficulty writing an essay each week. But in the spring, some students fell behind anyway.

I do not teach History 67 the same way today that I did when I began my career in college teaching. In the early-1970s I organized my version of this course around the argument that American society changed from being communal to individualistic between 1600 and 1877. This approach seemed to work well then, and its underlying idea remains a part of my teaching. But after being away from this course for several years I decided that I needed to revise my version of it around a broader and less abstract framework that would more readily engage today's sophomores and freshmen. I chose freedom, diversity, and migration as themes because these concepts are at least familiar if not transparent to most Americans. CPH67 represents an attempt to demonstrate how I now use these three themes to make this basic course more accessible to beginning college students.

Practical Lessons

A historian contemplating a course portfolio might want to know how much time it took me to put one together. I spent between one and two hours per week during the fall semester 1996 when I started preparing it from scratch. I devoted the bulk of that time to writing the course narrative, but assembling and organizing the syllabus, handouts, and other course materials also was time-consuming. Going into such depth and detail might burden the author, but it can benefit colleagues thinking about doing a course portfolio of their own or planning to teach a similar course for the first or second time. Course portfolios can serve both these functions; and, as a formative exercise, the time devoted to them can be justified not just because of their value to their authors but also because of what they can do to help others engaged in similar kinds of teaching.

As either a model for practice or a reflection on experimentation, the course portfolio need not be just a snapshot of someone's teaching. It can be an account of the ongoing narrative of the course over time. For instance, after the spring semester 1997 I wrote a short, reflective statement describing the different context of the History 67 section that I taught that term. It had a more diverse enrollment, including students from Ireland, Russia, and Vietnam, and was taught in 90-minute blocks (i.e., a Tuesday/Thursday schedule) that reduced the amount of lecture time because we devoted every other class to discussion.

Because I worked with a different TA each time, the tone of the course was also not the same. In each semester, my TA wrote the questions that we both used to frame the weekly class discussions. Compared with her counterpart in the fall, my spring TA encouraged students to be more structured and less open-ended in their thinking. In retrospect, I think this probably led to a subtle change in the nature of those conversations, which a reader of my portfolio could infer by comparing the two sets of discussion questions.

Examining Student Learning

Aside from documenting the scholarship of the instructor, a course portfolio can open the door to a careful consideration of student learning. It can help teachers of history (or any discipline) think more carefully about what their students are learning and how that learning relates to the content and methods of instruction. But a serious problem arises when it comes to documenting that learning, because the amount of written work done by students of history is large, and most readers of a history portfolio will not be able to read it all, even if they are so inclined.

I dealt with this problem in two

ways. First, my TAs and I wrote our midterm examination comments on the same floppy disk, a strategy that made it easy to include them in my portfolio. We spoke to what the students did both well and poorly on the exam and made a special effort to point out how the examination questions picked up on the three course themes. By consulting this relatively brief section of my portfolio, a reader would have no trouble getting a good idea about the extent to which my students demonstrated their command of these themes on the midterm.

Second, I asked my students in both semesters to write sample questions for their final examinations, promising them that I would use the best of the lot on the actual test. This assignment required them to make a judgment about what was important in the course. The questions they wrote let me know whether they had understood my priorities. Unfortunately, some wrote better questions for the final than they did answers on the actual examination.

I would recommend both of these strategies to anyone preparing a course portfolio in history, but it should be pointed out that they have their limitations. Neither strategy allows for the documentation of student development over time. This calls for monitoring the performance of students as they engage the material week to week. I addressed this need by tracking some of my students' journals and including those from the fall semester in a special appendix. More often than not, this exercise demonstrated that most students quickly establish a level of performance, good or bad, and stick to it throughout the semester.

This past term (fall 1997), when I taught History 67 again, I tried to help my students break out of this pattern by providing a higher level of feedback, week to week, on journal entries. I focused my comments on their use of historical data to support generalizations, a teaching strategy that seemed to help those who were academically in the middle compared with their stronger and weaker peers. The best students did not need such direction, while the poorest were not able to profit from it. Based on my experience with CPH67, I am prepared to say, in conclusion, that doing a course portfolio in history can provide both a learning and a teaching experience. I benefited by reflecting on content and method from term to term. I hope my readers have gained by learning something about how I teach a basic history course, a lesson that could be put to either a formative or a summative end.

Those interested in examining the portfolio itself can find it on the website of the American Historical Association located at http://chnm.gmu.edu/aha.

A Course Portfolio for a Graduate Nursing Course

Donna Martsolf, Nursing, Kent State University

"At next month's Graduate Curriculum Committee meeting, we would like to discuss the theory course. We've wanted to do this for several years and we're interested in knowing what you're teaching in that class."

These words, spoken by the chairperson of the Graduate Curriculum Committee (GCC) in Kent State's nursing program, directed at me as a first-year faculty member, definitely got my attention. I was well aware that my approach to Theoretical Basis of Nursing (N60101) was somewhat unorthodox, not the way the course is typically taught. Rather than a march through various theorists' thinking, my course was aimed at helping students understand the value of theory in reconceiving and shaping practice. And now I was going to have to defend my new approach.

In preparation for the next GCC meeting I developed a one-page handout that summarized the course description, objectives, and outline. At the meeting, I walked the faculty through the handout, explaining the thinking behind each aspect of the course as I conceived it. And then came the wonderful moment when a senior colleague — a recent hire — jumped into the discussion by stating, "I have taught this course at my former university. I know the literature in this area, and I believe strongly that this is exactly how this course should be taught." She went on to make a strong argument that other approaches to the course content

were not appropriate. Her argument for my approach, which was obviously hers as well, was strong and compelling, making points that were for me, at that time, mostly intuitive, not fully articulated.

The discussion ended with a recommendation for no change in the course. It was also the beginning of a journey that would eventually lead me to the development of a course portfolio for Theoretical Basis of Nursing.

A New View of Teaching

Shortly after the GCC experience, I was selected as one member of a two-person team from my program to participate in a national project on the peer review of teaching, sponsored by AAHE. In preparation for the first all-project meeting, held in June 1994 at Stanford University, I worked with my project partner on three "exercises" we had been asked to complete: writing reflective essays on a syllabus, on teaching methods, and on techniques for evaluating student work in a particular course. (Readers will find information about these assignments in the "Resources for Further Work" chapter in this volume.) The assignment was to focus on an undergraduate course, so I chose to focus on a course other than Theoretical Basis of Nursing, but it was in the back of my mind, even then.

At the Stanford meeting, I was introduced to Ernest L. Boyer's ideas about scholarship and its four forms. Thinking about teaching as a form of scholarship held great appeal for me. I really enjoyed teaching, and students had affirmed my teaching through their evaluations, but I had never considered investigating and reflecting on my own teaching in a more scholarly fashion. And the idea of using portfolios to undertake such investigation and to document growth and excellence in a career of teaching made sense to me. Because I was on the tenure track, I was well aware that idealistic notions about becoming a better teacher would only "count" if I could credibly document my progress and effectiveness. I therefore decided to try to construct a teaching portfolio that could be included as part of my reappointment folder for the following year.

From Teaching Portfolio to Course Portfolio

During three full, uninterrupted days between terms, I completed the teaching portfolio. From this exercise I learned again that reflection on teaching is very helpful in elevating one's teaching and in fostering planned change in courses. However, the process was unfulfilling in that a teaching portfolio, at least as I understood it, focuses on the best examples of one's scholarship of teaching; problematic aspects of teaching are not analyzed in depth, and so the potential for learning from mistakes is lost. The process of focusing on the best of my teaching in my short career seemed somehow artificial and contrived.

Moreover, the teaching portfolio's broad focus on teaching in multiple settings does not allow a more sustained focus on the conception and unfolding of a complete course from start to finish, which, I gradually realized, was something that held high interest for me. Thus, I jumped at the

chance when the AAHE project issued an invitation to faculty who wanted to experiment with a new genre of reflective teaching — the course portfolio. Here, it seemed, was a medium (or, as some people in the group called it, a "genre") through which I could reflect on the realities of constructing and enacting a course, with all of its pleasure and pain. With my past experience in arguing for my approach to Theoretical Basis of Nursing, the course portfolio piqued my interest.

Course Portfolio as Argument

The purpose of my particular course portfolio was to provide justification for the course design and pedagogical methods I used in Theoretical Basis. My original argument to the GCC provided the framework for a much more elaborated, carefully reflective critique in the course portfolio.

In particular, I was interested in uncovering and investigating what was for me the central organizing principle of the course, the aim of which, in my view, was to assist beginning graduate nursing students to change dramatically the way they think about nursing and the phenomenon of interest in nursing. The typical graduate student, in my experience, enters a master's program in nursing with a way of knowing that is particularistic, tradition-based, and focused on "doing" and the "bottom line."

The purpose of Theoretical Basis of Nursing as I teach it is to help this student begin to think abstractly, conceptualize, question, and wonder how and why. I was, therefore, curious about how and when students made the transition from particularistic to abstract thinking. Each time I taught the course, it seemed apparent in final papers and presentations that the transition had occurred. However, I had no real knowledge about how that change transpired, and I wanted to use the portfolio to explore this question and make a case for my approach.

I was most interested in making my case to my own colleagues at Kent State University, but I also saw the portfolio as a vehicle for explaining my still fairly unorthodox approach to the teaching of nursing theory to colleagues at the national level. It was my chance to contribute to the scholarship of teaching and learning within the professional community.

The Design of the Portfolio

The first draft of my portfolio began with background, including the syllabus, a record of the semesters in which I had taught the course, and the number of students enrolled.

Four sections followed, focused on course design, teaching the course, evaluating students, and my efforts to stay current with the field. Each of the four parts included relevant artifacts and a four- or five-page reflective essay.

In the first section, for example, I reflected on course design by making the argument that the course was designed to allow students gradually to acquire knowledge on theoretical thinking. To support this argument, I included artifacts such as the course calendar and the weekly discussion guides. In the section on teaching the course, my essay argued that students should be active learners of course content that, although theoretical in nature, should have significant practical application. Following the third essay on evaluating student work, I included copies of graded stu-

dent papers as evidence of my evaluation methods. In the final section of the portfolio, I reflected on the efforts that I had made to stay current in nursing theory. Future goals for the course were also listed in this section.

Revising the Portfolio

Since that first draft, the portfolio has undergone two revisions based on feedback from members of the AAHE Course Portfolio Working Group. After the first review, I made changes that were more cosmetic than substantive, adding a table of contents and a synopsis of the entire portfolio. These changes were made to assist the reader to "get around in the document" with ease and to allow for selective reading.

A second, more substantive revision involved adding the "student voice." In the earlier version of the portfolio, I had focused primarily on my *own* view of how the course unfolded. At the suggestion of the Working Group, I collected weekly feedback from the students about what they were learning, how that learning had occurred, and what difficulties they encountered in dealing with course content. This weekly feedback helped to illuminate my central question about how students move to a new, more abstract conception of the field. I included examples of all the students' responses at two points in the semester and one student's feedback every week. This revision added important evidence to the portfolio.

Costs and Benefits

The process of constructing a course portfolio is not painless. The thinking that was necessary for reflective writing and the construction of the document took time (probably 20 hours).

However, there are significant benefits to the process.

The primary benefit for me was the focus on student learning. Weekly student reflections, solicited in order to fill out the portfolio with relevant evidence, have helped me to clarify, and therefore more immediately address and correct, student misconceptions. As a result, student learning has occurred much more quickly this semester than it has in previous semesters. I have evidence that students understand the importance of theoretical thinking in nursing and that this understanding occurred as early as week five for some students and by week eight for all of them.

The second benefit is that the portfolio can be the basis for important discussion among groups of faculty who teach the same course. Two faculty members who teach other sections of this course read my portfolio. The argument that the course should focus on theoretical thinking rather than on specific theorists sparked lively discussion between the three of us since we had quite different views about this matter. However, through the process of discussion, we were able to construct one syllabus that could be used by any of us when assigned to teach the course. The discussion constituted a form of peer review that sent each of us to the recent literature and caused all of us to reexamine our ideas about the current state of theory in nursing.

Is It Worth It?

Faculty reactions when I share my work have been primarily of two kinds. Most faculty have been either excited or overwhelmed — or both. Faculty talk enthusiastically about taking time out from their teaching to reflect on the practice. They see great potential in the course portfolio to guide analysis and planned change in their courses. Discussing teaching problems and sharing solutions with other teachers elevates teaching to a true form of scholarship, and faculty get excited about that idea. Invariably, however, they express concern about finding time to engage in yet another activity with unproven return.

From my own experience, constructing a course portfolio made sense only when I had a compelling reason to do so. In the absence of such a reason, the course portfolio might well have been an exercise in wasted time. But the invitation to present my course to the GCC and the reappointment evaluation were two compelling reasons that made using my time for written reflection on teaching worthwhile indeed.

Why Now? Course Portfolios in Context[3]

*Mary Taylor Huber, Senior Scholar, The Carnegie Foundation for
the Advancement of Teaching*

Today's rising interest in course portfolios needs to be seen in three contexts. The first context is that of the scope of the term *scholarship*, as articulated in the Carnegie Foundation's report *Scholarship Reconsidered* (Boyer 1990). The second context concerns innovations in the documentation and review of teaching, especially those developed by Lee Shulman, Pat Hutchings, and their many collaborators among faculty and administrators under the auspices of AAHE's Teaching Initiatives. The third context, finally, is that of evaluation; in particular, I'd like to highlight Carnegie's follow-up report, *Scholarship Assessed* (Glassick, Huber, and Maeroff 1997).

The Scope of Scholarship

It was *Scholarship Reconsidered*, by Carnegie's late president Ernest L. Boyer, that put the idea of a "scholarship of teaching" on the map of higher education. The report proposed that colleges and universities need a fresh vision of scholarship in order to tap the full range of faculty talent. It concluded that institutions should broaden the scope of scholarship, setting out a view of scholarship as having four separate but overlapping dimensions: the scholarship of discovery, the scholarship of integration, the scholarship of application, and the scholarship of teaching. Boyer noted, too, however, that while these various types of scholarship are closely interrelated, the scholarly community's capacity to support, report, and evaluate them has been wildly uneven.

Drawing on *Scholarship Reconsidered* and *Scholarship Assessed*, let me quickly review the argument. The first and most familiar element in this model — the scholarship of discovery — comes closest to what academics mean when they speak of "research," although this type of scholarship also includes the creative work of faculty in the literary, visual, and performing arts. The academy holds no tenet in higher regard than the pursuit of knowledge for its own sake, a determination to give free rein to fair and honest inquiry, wherever it may lead. At its best, the scholarship of discovery contributes not only to the stock of human knowledge but also to the intellectual climate of a college or university. The process, the outcomes, and especially the passion of discovery enhance the meaning of the effort and of the institution itself. The question behind this kind of scholarship is, What do I know and how do I know it?, and the scholarly community has very well established traditions for reporting and evaluating results.

Integration, the second of the four forms of scholarship, involves faculty members in overcoming the isolation and fragmentation of disciplines. The scholarship of integration makes connections within and between disciplines, altering the contexts in which people view knowledge and offsetting the inclination to split knowledge into ever more esoteric bits and pieces. Often, inte-

---

[3]*An earlier version of this essay was presented at the Annual Meeting of the American Historical Association, Seattle, Washington, January 1998.*

grative scholarship educates nonspecialists by giving meaning to isolated facts and putting them in perspective. The scholarship of integration seeks to interpret, draw together, and bring new insight to bear on original research. The key question here is not so much, What is known? but, What does it mean? And the scholarly community has well-established ways of dealing with this kind of scholarship — when it is addressed to disciplinary or even interdisciplinary colleagues. In my field, anthropology, genres such as "review articles" and "introductions to edited volumes" can be as highly regarded as articles reporting one's original research. (Of course it helps if the journal is prestigious and the author well known.)

When it comes to integrative scholarship aimed at public audiences, the situation is less certain. "Popularizers" have not always found praise (or even serious critique) in their disciplinary homes. And when genres expand beyond print, to film and museum exhibits, for example, many academics do not have an appropriate critical vocabulary ready at hand, and many are perplexed by the problem of sorting out the scholar's contribution to such complex professional collaborations. As a result, "public scholarship" has often been discouraged in colleges and universities by the lack of recognition and reward (see Huber 1997).

These first two kinds of scholarship — the discovery and the integration of knowledge — reflect the investigative and synthesizing traditions of academic life. The third element, the application of knowledge, moves toward engagement, as the scholar asks, How can knowledge be responsibly applied to consequential problems? Higher learning in this country has long been viewed as being useful "in the nation's service," as Woodrow Wilson famously put it (1961). Yet this obligation to the larger society goes beyond Wilson's vision of educating future leaders. Colleges and universities understand that their "service" mission means responding to the issues of the day, following the model set in place more than a century ago by the land-grant colleges as they tried to meet the needs of the nation's farmers. Lessons learned in the application of knowledge can enrich teaching, and new intellectual understandings can arise from the very act of application, whether in medical diagnosis, exploration of an environmental problem, study of a design defect in architecture, or an attempt to apply the latest learning theories in public schools. Theory and practice interact in such ventures and improve each other.

Or so one hopes. As anyone knows who has engaged in the scholarship of application, these scholarly virtues are not always easy to convey to one's colleagues (see Lynton 1995). Applied scholarship often results in reports to one's clients. In public history, as Kendrick Clements notes, these reports may include "strange-looking materials like environmental impact statements, museum displays, or historic structure reports" (1988, 6) — not the stuff around which departmental evaluations usually revolve. Michael Berube, of the University of Illinois at Urbana-Champaign, puts it this way: "If I am going to be a responsible professional and professor, I make my work available to the clients of my university and of my discipline; to some extent — as a teacher, as a citizen, as a professional — I take the shape of my container" (1996, 17). With applied scholarship, that container is not always the easy-to-review article or book, and this has hampered the development of applied work, especially in the liberal arts and sciences.

Finally, we come to the scholarship of teaching, which initiates students into the best values of the academy, engaging them in new fields of study and thus — it is hoped — enabling them to understand and participate more fully in the larger culture. Teaching, in this view, is not simply a matter of method and technique, but a matter of selecting, organizing, and transforming one's field in ways that connect with students' diverse mental worlds (see Hutchings 1996, 1). To see teaching as scholarship is to recognize that the work of the professor becomes consequential only as it is understood by others — in this case, students. But not only students, because the scholarship of teaching, like other kinds of scholarship, should cumulate, add up, and contribute to the practice of one's colleagues. Seen in this way, the work of teaching — as Lee Shulman has argued — rightly belongs to and requires a community of scholars (1993).

The idea of a "scholarship of teaching" was well received in the early-1990s, perhaps because it held out a hand to an enterprise troubled by a familiar litany of problems. For starters, most faculty have had no training as teachers, and graduate programs are only beginning to change this historical reality. Second, teaching has not counted for much in the faculty reward system, especially on the research university campuses that tend to shape the ambitions of higher education more generally. Third, teaching has been the most difficult to evaluate, in part because it has been so hard to "make public." Indeed, there are still relatively few forums in which faculty in history, or anthropology, or mathematics, or chemistry can meet to discuss teaching and build up some common knowledge and a critical discourse about it.

The Documentation and Review of Teaching

This is where the second context for understanding course portfolios comes in: the recent rapid pace of innovation in reporting, documenting, and evaluating teaching. I want to emphasize here that teaching is not alone. Advocates of integrative and applied scholarship have also come forward to enhance their visibility and legitimacy in academe. Indeed, the dimensions of interest on campuses in the early- to mid-1990s are indicated by a 1994 survey of chief academic officers at all of the country's four-year colleges and universities. Some 80 percent of responding provosts reported that their institutions either had recently reexamined their systems of faculty roles and rewards or planned to do so, and the most widely embraced goal of these reviews was to redefine such traditional faculty roles as teaching, research, and service (Glassick, Huber, and Maeroff 1997, 12). Many scholarly associations, including the American Historical Association, the Joint Policy Board for Mathematics, the Association of American Geographers, and the American Chemical Society, have revised their statements of professional work to embrace more than published monographs and refereed articles that report on original research (Diamond and Adam 1995). National meetings on related topics have also drawn increasing attention: AAHE's annual conference of its Forum on Faculty Roles & Rewards grew from 564 participants at the first meeting in 1993 to more than 1,000 in 1997 and 1998. As R. Eugene Rice, director of the Forum, observed, "New issues related to the changing priorities, rewards, and responsibilities of the professoriate are drawn to our attention almost daily. Hundreds of campus projects designed to address these issues are now in place and examples of good practice are readily available" (1995, 1).

Innovation in the documentation and review of teaching has certainly led the field. Some of this, to be sure, was driven by a simple concern to move beyond excessive reliance on student evaluations in the assessment of teaching. But some of it was driven by a desire to encourage what Russell Edgerton (then president of AAHE) called "a culture of interest in teaching" that would "contain its own dynamic for continual improvement" (1996, vi). AAHE's Teaching Initiatives decided to do this by experimenting with documentation that would "introduce faculty to a conception of teaching that honored faculty's intuitive appreciation for the subtle processes of 'knowledge transformation' entailed in quality teaching" (Edgerton 1996, vi). Teaching portfolios were an early and popular innovation, but more recently AAHE coordinated a national project on the peer review of teaching, on which this volume draws, exploring a variety of ways to make teaching what Shulman calls "community property" (1993). Another recent AAHE publication, *Making Teaching Community Property*, gives a "menu" of strategies for encouraging peer collaboration and review, including teaching circles for starting the conversation in academic departments; reciprocal visits and observations in the classroom; mentoring; focusing on student learning; portfolios; collaborative inquiry and pedagogical scholarship; departmental occasions for collaboration (from pedagogical colloquia during the hiring process, to TA training, to departmental teaching libraries); and last but not least, intercampus collaboration (often through the Internet) and the external review of teaching (Hutchings 1996).

This exploration of strategies for documenting and sharing teaching is a key context in which the course portfolio has developed. Unlike a teaching portfolio, which, as Pat Hutchings says, "represents a broad sampling of the faculty member's pedagogical work — in a variety of different courses, over a number of years," the course portfolio zeroes in on "the unfolding of a single course, from conception to results" (1996, 50-51).

Why this focus on the course? Other chapters and the case studies in this volume provide a rationale for the course portfolio, and my own analysis overlaps with what others say. The first rationale lies in the fact that the course is both the most common "unit" of teaching and the most strategic, because it is "within the course that knowledge of the field intersects with knowledge about particular students and their learning" (Hutchings 1996, 51). The second is the conviction that courses, like research, are acts of intellectual invention, and that the way in which one teaches a course enacts the way one thinks about and pursues one's field of study (Carnegie 1997). Third is the conclusion of practitioners, documented in this volume, that the course portfolio can be an excellent tool for reflecting on and improving one's teaching. And a fourth is the faith that — as Shulman puts it — the course portfolio can powerfully "inform other members of the community" and engage them in conversation and critique (Shulman et al. 1996, 11).

The Course Portfolio and the Evaluation of Scholarly Work

The third and final context in which I would place course portfolios is the evaluation of scholarly work. And here I'd like to underline that course portfolios such as those described in this volume are structured in a way that presents teaching as a familiar kind of scholarly project. William Cerbin, a psychologist at the University of Wisconsin-La Crosse and pioneer of course portfolios, describes the origin of the idea as an analogy to the investigative traditions of his discipline:

> *Being a social scientist, I began to think of each course ... as a kind of laboratory — not as a truly controlled experiment, of course, but as a setting in which you start out with goals for student learning, then you adopt teaching practices that you think will accomplish these, and along the way you can watch and see if your practices are helping to accomplish your goals, collecting evidence about effects and impact.*
>
> *In this sense, each course is a kind of discrete entity with a beginning and an end, fairly discrete goals you're trying to accomplish, and, typically, a body of content you're trying to deal with.*
>
> *So the course portfolio was a natural way to go. ... I'm not sure I saw this immediately, but one thing I now see is that the course portfolio is really like a scholarly manuscript ... a draft, of ongoing inquiry.* (1996, 53)

To people in other fields, the look and feel of a course portfolio might be somewhat different. For example, Steve Dunbar, a mathematician at the University of Nebraska-Lincoln, thinks of analogies to modes of representation in his own field:

> *When I get done I'm going to have something fewer than 50 pages — maybe closer to 30 — that I can give to colleagues to assess ... for mathematical content and validity of data: Were my goals good goals? Did I actually meet these goals? ... [R]eviewers can analyze the portfolio as they would a piece of research. [It will be] comprehensive and data-based in a way that people haven't often seen.* (1996, 57-58)

As I'm sure you can imagine, a course portfolio by an English professor, an anthropologist, or a historian might look quite different. Indeed, Lee Shulman tells me that one mathematician, on seeing a historian's portfolio, was intrigued and delighted by the idea of couching such an account less in numbers than in narrative!

These themes of crossovers between different types of scholarly projects (research and teaching) and different disciplinary traditions were also picked up in *Scholarship Assessed*. In that report, my coauthors and I argued that it is indeed possible to evaluate all four kinds of scholarship — discovery, integration, application, and teaching — by similar criteria, as long as their documentation enables one to focus on the scholarly process itself. After all, one can ask of any project whether it had:

- clear and important goals,

- adequate preparation and selection of materials,

- appropriate methods,

- significant results,

- effective presentation,

- and whether it was subject to reflective critique (see Glassick, Huber, and Maeroff 1997, 36).

One of the great virtues of course portfolios, I think, is that they allow teaching to be represented in the form of a discrete project that can be examined in the same terms as other scholarly projects — thus highlighting the scholarship in teaching, and connecting it with scholarship in its other guises and forms.

As a new genre, the potential of the course portfolio remains to be fully explored. Certainly, it is a way of prompting and organizing a scholar's own reflections on teaching and learning of a specific topic by specific students in a specific context. Done well, a course portfolio can also be a way of archiving the experience and making it available to others. Still, course portfolios come in different degrees of polish. To use an analogy from cultural anthropology, some may be more like fieldnotes and others, more carefully crafted, like ethnographies. In the not-too-distant future, the most accessible course portfolios may even become a "literature" that scholars can consult and cite as they explore consequential issues in college and university teaching.

"I was most interested in making my case to my own colleagues at Kent State University, but I also saw the portfolio as a vehicle for explaining my still fairly unorthodox approach to the teaching of nursing theory to colleagues at the national level. It was my chance to contribute to the scholarship of teaching and learning within the professional community."

DONNA MARTSOLF
(THIS VOLUME, 27)

A Course Portfolio for a Colloquium in 20th-Century American Foreign Relations

Mary Ann Heiss, History, Kent State University

My course portfolio examines the execution of Colloquium on U.S. Foreign Relations (History 4/5/78097), a mixed undergraduate and graduate reading colloquium at Kent State University. Through individual and common readings and class discussions, the course introduces students to the major historiographical schools and debates that have marked the field. In addition to exposing students to a wide variety of literature, the course focuses on the different ways that historians approach their craft; how they use different sources or ask different questions of the same sources; and how they attempt to address the work of their predecessors.

Because the course emphasizes historiography, student work consists primarily of book reviews, which are a central feature of my portfolio. The undergraduates in the class had the chance to rewrite their first three reviews based on my comments, and I include samples of their first and second drafts to demonstrate their improvement. Students also were required to write a summary essay synthesizing all of the books that they had read, and I include samples of those papers, as well.

The Course and Its Students

My portfolio focuses on the course as I taught it during the spring 1997 semester. It met Tuesday evenings from 7:00 to 9:30 and enrolled 14 undergraduates, one M.A. student, and three Ph.D. students. (Four of the undergraduates eventually dropped the course; a fifth took an incomplete for the course and has yet to finish the work.) The large number of undergraduates made this course different from the last colloquium I taught, particularly in the way the class discussions proceeded. Many of the undergraduates were not used to a course that required significant class participation, that did not rely on a textbook, and that presupposed a general knowledge of the subject matter of the course. Over time, though, many of them rose to the occasion.

The undergraduate level of the course satisfies the university's writing-intensive requirement for majors, and most of the undergraduates in the class indicated that they were taking the class to satisfy the writing requirement. (The writing-intensive requirement's provision for guided revision of some student writing prompted my decision to have the undergraduates rewrite their first three reviews based upon my comments.) Most of the undergraduates eventually met the high reading and discussion demands of the course and did better than I think even they expected. A few, in fact, were outstanding students, who really added a lot to the class.

The Design and Unfolding of the Course

When deciding on the syllabus and organization of this course, I drew upon both the colloquia I had as a graduate student and advice from departmental colleagues. What I ended up with was a hybrid that combined what I considered the best features of both. From courses I had taken I borrowed the idea of including common readings for each week, particularly historiographical essays that would place the limited number of titles we read in class in the context of the other literature on that specific subject.

From those courses I also pulled the idea of having each individual student read different books so that the class would be exposed to literature that they had not read themselves but that they would nevertheless learn about from class discussions and an exchange of book reviews. Based on discussions with my colleagues about their experiences teaching a colloquium, however, I also set aside some weeks when all members of the class would read the same book. (For these weeks I chose books that were either on the cutting edge of the literature or considered classics.) Thus, the colloquium examined in this portfolio combines four weeks of common book readings with 10 weeks when students were to choose their reading from a list of titles that I provided.

That this course relied on a discussion format rather than lecture, which meant that it did not follow a specific, preplanned script each week, made documenting what transpired throughout the semester somewhat difficult. I utilized weekly teaching diary entries to record what I believed happened during discussions, and I included samples of students' book reviews to demonstrate their progress — admittedly uneven and faltering at times — in grappling with the literature that they were confronting.

My comments on the students' reviews were generally designed to prod them into identifying a book's thesis, assessing its argument, and seeing its place within the historiography — all of which fit in with the goals of the course as stated in the syllabus. Interpretations and arguments were the things I stressed during our class discussions, so that students would understand that it was how the books related to one another, not necessarily the specifics of their coverage, that was most important. As my diary entries reveal, some weeks my efforts in this regard were more successful than others.

Reflecting on the weekly progress of the course was definitely a valuable experience, as it afforded me the kind of introspection that can only come from putting one's thoughts into words. It did not take all that much time, so it was not much of a burden, and was most assuredly time well spent.

Examining Student Progress

Copying and assembling the students' weekly reviews for the portfolio was a more daunting task, as was choosing which papers to include for each week of the course. (Here my choices were often somewhat arbitrary, guided at times by nothing more than whimsy.) Yet putting everything together so that I could see the students' work in its entirety — from the rough and oftentimes uninspiring initial reviews to the fairly sophisticated and perceptive critiques that students were able to make by the end of the semester — illustrated in bold relief just how much progress most of the students made over the term, especially one or two individuals who were somewhat apprehensive about taking a course of this nature. Had I not gathered all of this material, I would probably not appreciate today how much progress some of the students had made by the end of the semester.

Lessons Learned

After rereading my weekly diary comments and reflecting on how the course turned out, I have concluded that I probably should have provided the undergraduates with more guidance, both orally in class and in the form of study questions or important ideas to look for in the literature. (I employed the study question approach in a course I taught during the fall 1997 term, and it worked quite well.) Because many of the undergraduates were unfamiliar with the material, they sometimes had a tendency to want to focus on the events covered in the books, rather than on the particulars and nuances of an author's argument. More guidance to help students know what to look for in the literature is something I will have to provide in the future.

The portfolio also highlighted for me the tendency of some of our discussions to be more event-oriented than I would have liked; this, I believe, had a detrimental effect on how much the graduate students were able to get out of the class. Some of the undergraduates' book reviews, though good when judged at the appropriate level of assessment, did not provide the graduate students with deep analysis, which defeated the purpose of having students exchange papers with one another. I'm afraid that in the end, the graduate students did not get the kind of book reviews that they can really use

to prepare for comprehensive exams.

In the future, I will no longer teach the colloquium with a mixed enrollment. I will teach either only undergraduates looking to satisfy the university's writing-intensive requirement or only graduate students. That way, each level of student can get the maximum benefit from the class. (In fact, the colloquium I taught on early American foreign relations during the spring 1998 semester was open only to graduate students.)

New Insights About My Field and the Teaching of It

Along with forcing me to think more about how to make the course better for my students, putting together this portfolio has renewed my appreciation for the links between the different books in my field. My own graduate training was highly historiographical, with a lot of emphasis on how books related to one another and how different historians were connected. Sitting down and writing up each week of this course has allowed me to see these links with fresh eyes. It has also made me actually think about why I made the choices I did in structuring the course, choosing the literature, and guiding the discussions. These are things I did instinctively, without really stopping to think of why.

Compiling the teaching diary made me think about and justify things I had previously simply done. This was especially helpful to me, as a junior faculty member not so far removed from her own graduate school experience. With relatively little to compare my own teaching against, it was helpful to actually sit down and ask myself why I structured the course as I did.

Setting out on paper my sense of how the course unfolded also made me think about just what in the field of U.S. diplomatic history I considered most important. What did I consider the major questions and debates? What books did I consider most significant or influential? Did my reactions to certain books — both now and when I had read them as a graduate student — square with the impressions of my own students? The choices I made when structuring my course said a lot about how I approached my own field. I certainly knew this when I compiled the syllabus for the course, but I had not stopped to consider what my choices really meant. (And here I should add that my teaching diary entries could probably stand to be more reflective in this respect.)

In any event, actually contemplating the reasons I constructed the course as I did was like writing my own historical account of how the field has developed, what I see as its most important and interesting debates, and why I think studying it is worthwhile.

Benefits for the Future

Compiling this portfolio has also provided me with a benchmark for comparing this course with other colloquia that I will teach in the future. When I teach one with the same topical coverage, I can make use of my teaching diary to recall which books worked and which did not, what kinds of things students found most interesting and perplexing, and where I might improve on my in-class explanations. Additionally, I can compare the written work of the students in last spring's course with that of future students. The diary entries will also prove helpful when I teach colloquia in the future to undergraduates. This is, of course, a different kind of teaching than running a graduate-level colloquium, and I will be better prepared for the next one I teach as a result of having compiled this portfolio.

For me, constructing the portfolio was a positive and very helpful exercise. It allowed me to think about why I ran my course as I did, provided me with a permanent record of each class session, and showed me ways to make the course better. As with any first-time endeavor, there are things about the portfolio that are less than perfect. It would benefit from student feedback about how the course was going — perhaps minute papers on the class discussions or midterm student evaluations. And I can see with hindsight that the teaching diary entries could stand more analysis in spots. Still, I believe that I have a better sense of my course from having completed the portfolio, and I believe that readers of it have a pretty good idea of what I tried to accomplish and whether I succeeded.

I compiled a similar document for the graduate-level colloquium I taught this past semester. Although it was a different kind of course than the one I taught last spring — a fact that will make direct comparisons impossible — keeping the teaching diary and collating the students' written work still proved a valuable experience.

I would recommend the portfolio approach to others, as well. It has given me the chance to see my teaching as a much more intellectual enterprise than I had earlier, given me a new appreciation for the exciting nature of my field, and ultimately made me a more thoughtful instructor. It was most assuredly worth the time investment.

A Course Portfolio in Mathematics

Orin Chein, Mathematics, Temple University

In some sense, my involvement with portfolios dates back to the spring of 1990, long before I had even heard the term. At that time, my service as department chair was coming to an end, and for a number of reasons (none of which had anything to do with superior knowledge about the art of teaching) the dean had selected me as the new director of the College of Arts and Sciences Teaching Improvement Center. I had always taken pride in the belief that I was a good teacher, but, as is the case with most college teachers, I had no formal training in teaching. I knew nothing about teaching theory or developmental frameworks, and so I attended a variety of conferences and workshops on the subject as preparation for my new position. At these, I learned many things; in particular, I became familiar with the notion of a teaching portfolio. When I was nominated, several years later, for Temple University's Great Teacher Award, I put this new knowledge to work by developing my own teaching portfolio (and was selected for the award).

I mention all this because I think it is relevant to why I became involved with a group of colleagues assembled by AAHE in a project to explore a new version — a subset really — of the teaching portfolio, "the course portfolio." Having already had a successful experience with the teaching portfolio, I was eager to join others in exploring this related form of documentation.

Choosing the Course

I knew from the start the course I would choose as a focus for my port-folio. Basic Concepts of Mathematics (Math 141) was a course that I had developed and introduced into the curriculum many years before, during my first few years at Temple, and one that had quickly become a requirement for all math majors. However, for two antipodal reasons, not all of my departmental colleagues were as convinced as I was of the importance of this requirement. Some felt the course was superfluous, because students eventually learn the same material when they take other courses. Others thought that the course was important but that it didn't go far enough in achieving its goals (to teach students how to think and write mathematically; to present topics that reappear often in later courses; to provide students with an early indicator of whether or not mathematics is really the field for them).

In any case, Basic Concepts of Mathematics was a course that had become identified with me more than any other in the curriculum, and it seemed the natural one to choose. As I write in my introductory remarks to the portfolio,

> *By preparing this portfolio, I can showcase exactly how I think this course should be taught, what it should cover, what should be emphasized, how different aspects of the course hang together. This prepares a foundation on which further discussion and negotiation with my colleagues can be based.*

Thinking About Purposes

As noted above, I undertook the process of developing my course portfolio as part of a group of colleagues from around the country. At one of our early meetings, we discussed two essential questions: What should go into a course portfolio? and Why would a person want to develop a course portfolio? We decided that the answer to the former question might well depend on the answer to the latter, and we then identified three primary reasons that one might want to develop a portfolio: for use in personnel decisions, as a pedagogical tool, and as an introspective tool. Each of us agreed to develop our portfolio along one of these lines, but I decided to keep all three purposes in mind.

Although I already was a tenured full professor and I had received an award for the quality of my teaching, I thought that preparing a course portfolio might prove useful for future personnel decisions. Our collective bargaining agreement with the university allocates a pool of money annually for merit awards, and merit for teaching is one category for which those awards are made. I thought that developing this portfolio might be useful in supporting a case I might make for such an award. I also was considering applying for a different teaching award (from the College of Arts and Sciences, rather than from the university as a whole), and I thought the course portfolio might be helpful for that, as well.

The pedagogical usefulness of this portfolio is evident in the reasons for which I decided to focus on Basic Concepts of Mathematics, as noted above. I saw the portfolio as a vehicle through which I could make a case for why this is an important course — possibly the most important course

in our curriculum. It also gave me an opportunity to present my own thinking about how the course should be taught. I was eager to do this because I believe that at least part of the criticism from those who feel that the course does not do enough to prepare students for some of our more advanced courses can be attributed to the fact that not everyone who teaches the course (at least 10 different people have taught it in recent years) emphasizes what I consider to be the appropriate topics or covers everything that I think the course should cover.

(Now that I write this, I realize that although my portfolio, in its current version, usefully presents *what* I cover when I teach the course, it needs to say more about *why*. I mention this to make the point that a course portfolio is a living document, one that can be revised or embellished as often as one feels inclined to do so.)

The third reason for developing a portfolio — its usefulness as a tool for introspection — has turned out to be the most important one for me. I have had to examine my goals in teaching this course and the ways in which I hope to accomplish them. In the process of doing so, I developed a number of new teaching tools and techniques. Unfortunately, most of the work on my portfolio took place after the fall of 1995. As I did not have an opportunity to teach this course again until the fall of 1997, I was not able to put some of my new ideas to the immediate test in this course. However, I was able to experiment with some of them in other courses. I am pleased by the results and plan to continue using the ideas in appropriate courses in the future. I will discuss some of these further below.

Starting With Reflection

During the fall of 1995, I taught Basic Concepts and immediately began the process of developing my course portfolio. My first task was to write a reflective statement in which I discuss my goals when I teach the course and what I try to accomplish, how I conduct the class and why, my view of the role of a teacher, my philosophy of homework and testing, and a number of innovations and experiments I planned to try, especially to attempt to get the students more actively involved in the learning process. Writing the reflective statement also provided me with an opportunity to expand and elaborate on the syllabus I distribute to the class so that students can know exactly what will be expected of them and so they can acquire in advance a fuller appreciation of what the course is about.

Sampling Student Work

Having evaluated some of our in-progress early drafts, my colleagues and I in the AAHE Course Portfolio Working Group all agreed that a portfolio should include samples of actual student work. But the question was how much. Since my course is an intensive writing (IW) offering (that is, it is one of a number of courses at the university that satisfies a writing-across-the-curriculum requirement), students are required to do a considerable amount of writing. This includes not only several examinations and a group term paper but also regular weekly homework assignments and occasional revisions, as well.

As a result, I collect a large amount of written material from my students. I included much of this in the student work section of the first draft of my portfolio. I included the actual student papers with my comments about what was wrong, what was well done, suggestions for rewriting, etc. (I returned this work to students as it was corrected throughout the semester, but I collected it again in a student portfolio at the semester's end.)

When the Working Group met in the fall of 1996 to exchange draft portfolios, it was generally agreed that mine was too bulky and that only a sampling of student work should be included. But how should that sampling be selected? Should it be the best work of the best students, or should it be selected from the whole spectrum of student performance? And how large a sample should be included? While we never really reached agreement on the latter issue, we did agree that one approach to this problem would be to identify a random sample of students at the beginning of the course and to include their work in the portfolio.

The Question of Quality

During the discussions of the Working Group, it became clear that one of the issues we would have to address (at least for portfolios intended for use in personnel decisions) is the question of quality: How, that is, do our portfolios present evidence of and allow judgments about teaching effectiveness? Student evaluations, which can be included in our portfolios, give evidence of what our students think of our teaching ability and approach, but they don't present evidence of what the students have learned. Samples of student work, including homework, term papers, and/or examinations (the kind of things I included in my portfolio) provide more direct evidence about student learning, but drawing conclusions about the quality of teaching is nevertheless problematic, especially for readers from outside the field.

For teachers who regularly teach multi-section courses, effectiveness might be assessed through the use of uniform final examinations, with comparisons of student performance made over a period of several years, rather than based on a single semester. For those teaching introductory courses, effectiveness might be measured by tracing student performance in subsequent courses. But neither of these approaches was practical in my situation. Instead, I settled on several techniques that I have now incorporated into all of my other courses, as well. These assessment techniques are described in detail in my portfolio, but I will simply summarize them here.

1. At the beginning of the semester, I administer a pre-test on which I list all the terms and concepts I hope to discuss during the course of the semester. Using a five-point scale ranging from "never heard of it" to "understand it well enough to teach it to someone else," students are to rate their confidence in their knowledge of each topic. The same test is then administered at the end of the semester (as a post-test), and the results are compared. (Students were assured that their performance on these "tests" had no bearing whatsoever on their grades.) A discussion of this comparison is included in the portfolio.

2. After each class, each student is required to prepare an index card in accordance with a format described in the course syllabus. These index cards are collected weekly to provide me with a picture of what students think they are learning or what they think they do not really understand. They also provide students with an occasional opportunity to display their grasp of the "big picture" in mathematics. I return these cards to the students, with my comments and suggestions, and then I collect them again at the end of the semester. I included a sample of these cards in the portfolio because they not only give a picture of what students learned, they also help illuminate how I teach.

3. At the end of the semester, again in accordance with specific instructions contained in the course syllabus, students are required to write a brief (two-page) paper summarizing what they feel the course was about and what they learned. These summaries are included in the portfolio.

4. Students are also required to write a description of their group experience and an evaluation of the other members of their group, following a framework of specific questions that I put forth. These, too, now appear in the portfolio.

These assessment strategies do not, I'm aware, completely and unambiguously answer all questions about quality, but they are surely an improvement over the current prevailing dependence on student satisfaction ratings alone. I feel that my portfolio gives a much more complete and reliable picture of the effects of the course on students' learning than I was able to achieve without it.

The Impact of the Portfolio on Teaching Practice

In addition to motivating me to adopt some of the assessment techniques discussed above, working on the course portfolio has led to several other innovations in my teaching. As a result of having to examine exactly what I would like students to get out of the course, I have collected a list of terms, theorems, and techniques that I would like them to know and master. I have turned this list into a study guide, which I now distribute to my class. (I have subsequently done the same for other courses, as well.)

As I mentioned above, because this is an IW course I have always required a substantial amount of writing on the part of my students. As a result of my work on the portfolio, I have rethought my role in helping students develop their writing skills. I have restructured some assignments and added others. Students now have to rewrite and resubmit several of their weekly writing assignments. At the end of the semester, they have to submit a portfolio containing their best and most improved work, as well as their weekly index cards and several other items. In addition, each week two students in the class serve as class secretaries. They write up the notes for the week and submit them to me for comment and correction. They then have to rewrite them for ultimate distribution to the class.

Finally, students have to participate in a group project that requires them to write a paper on material that time constraints have prevented me from covering in class. Samples of this collaborative student work are contained in my portfolio.

Group work is another area in which my teaching has been developing. While I started experimenting with group projects even before the AAHE project, I did so with only limited success. Many of the better students resent "wasting their time" when they feel they would be more efficient and just as successful working on their own. Groups with primarily weaker students often flounder around, having no idea where to start or how to continue even if I help them get started. Nevertheless, I fully believe that active learning results in better understanding and longer retention.

I continued to think about these issues as I worked on my portfolio, and I decided that what is needed are well-designed "discovery" exercises, which actively involve the students in discovering new results for themselves and which students can attack as individuals or in a group, as they see fit. Designing such exercises is not easy, and none was available when my portfolio was last assembled. This semester I have developed a few so far, and I will include them in my next edition of the portfolio.

The Time Commitment

One of the questions I am asked most frequently is how long it took me to assemble my course portfolio. Truthfully, I do not know the answer. I would say that I certainly spent in excess of 50 hours, and maybe even as many as 100. However, this includes not only the time I spent writing introductory remarks and my reflective statement but also the time I spent expanding the syllabus, developing the study guides, creating and analyzing pre- and post-tests, developing discovery exercises, and doing the many rewrites that resulted from my evolving sense of what would make the portfolio (as well as the course) most effective. With one course portfolio now under my belt, I think I will be able to complete my second one (which I plan to do soon) in much less time — maybe as few as 20 hours.

Responses From Readers

A question of concern common to many of us developing course portfolios is, How can we make portfolios most helpful to readers, especially to those who might use them to help make personnel decisions? Aside from creating a good table of contents and using separators and color-coding and the like, the real question is, What should the portfolio contain to make it readable and useful to someone who might have to read many such portfolios? We agreed that the portfolio needed "narrative glue" to make it readable; that is, it had to tell the story of the course. But we also wanted to know what sense readers would make of this story.

To answer this question, I selected three people from my institution who agreed to read my portfolio: my department chair, the chair of the College Personnel Committee, and the provost. Along with my portfolio (sans student work), I sent each of them the following set of questions:

1. Does the portfolio provide you with insight into the way I teach this course? What else would you need to see in order to get such insight?

2. If you were on a search committee or a promotions and tenure committee or an awards committee, would this portfolio help you judge the quality of my performance as a teacher? What if your field of interest or expertise had no relationship to the course in question? If many or all candidates under review by such a committee were to submit portfo-

lios such as this, would that present a problem? If so, do you have any suggestions?

3. If you were assigned to teach this course for the first time, would reading this portfolio be helpful to you?

4. Would a portfolio such as this be useful to make an argument about the value of a course such as this and/or the way in which it should be taught?

5. What, if anything, could be done to make the portfolio more accessible? Is there material that should be omitted or additional material that should be included? Should the portfolio be organized differently? Would a cover sheet of guidelines for the reader be helpful?

6. With regard to samples of student work, would it have been helpful to you if I had included some with the material I sent you? Should they be included with an actual portfolio?

7. Do you have any additional comments or suggestions that would be helpful?

As of this writing, I have received only one response — from the provost, who happens to be a mathematician (and who has since left the institution). In his written feedback to me, he said that the portfolio reveals much about the course and how I teach it, but that he was not sure that he had learned enough to form an opinion with regard to the controversy concerning the place of the course in the curriculum. He suggested that a clearer statement of the goals of the course and how these goals relate to the rest of the mathematics curriculum would be helpful.

The provost reports that the elements of the portfolio that he found most useful were "the extremely detailed syllabus"; the supplementary exercises and exams, which "showed the range of mathematics you included in the course, as well as what a successful student should be able to do at the end of the course"; and the pre- and post-tests together with the results. He added that with some examples of student work (which I had not included in what I provided, but do appear in the actual portfolio), the portfolio should "go a long way towards helping make a good evaluation of the quality of teaching and the amount of student learning in this course."

Additionally, the provost suggested that one item about which he would have liked more information was the question of whether I had experimented with different cooperative learning techniques, and if so, how well each of these techniques worked. His final remark was that he was "relieved by the length of [the] portfolio." He said he had feared that "the volume of paper per portfolio would overwhelm my capacity to deduce useful information from them." Apparently, this proved not to be the case (although I can't help wondering whether he would still feel the same way if 20 people had simultaneously submitted portfolios for his perusal).

Conclusion

As you may surmise from the opening section of this case study, the history of my involvement with the course portfolio is closely tied to my own personal circumstances and interests. I do not claim that others would have my experience. Nevertheless, judging from the case studies of my colleagues whose work is represented here, I believe that the personal growth and development I experienced is likely to be shared by any readers of this volume who are willing to devote the time and effort needed to develop a course portfolio of their own.

way it does and why my take on the course is an appropriate one for my students and my goals. This opening syllabus-plus-reflection is in some ways the most important section in the portfolio, in that it sets the context for everything that follows.

Documenting Enactment

Naturally, the portfolio needs to capture not only the intentions behind the course and its design but also what actually *happens* as the course unfolds. What goes on in class? What do students do? How is class time (and homework time) spent? Though this in-class aspect of teaching is typically what people think of when they think of teaching, it is in some ways the most frustrating aspect of portfolio development in that there are so many options and possibilities . . . and so little sense of which of the many items that might be included are most useful, in what combination, and in what level of detail. Mary Ann Heiss notes in case study 3, for instance, that reliance on a "discussion format rather than lecture, which meant that [the course] did not follow a specific, preplanned script each week, made documenting what transpired throughout the semester somewhat difficult" (36). Her solution was to keep a weekly teaching diary, as part of the portfolio development process: "Reflecting on the weekly progress of the course was definitely a valuable experience, as it afforded me the kind of introspection that can only come from putting one's thoughts into words. It did not take all that much time, so it was not much of a burden, and was most assuredly time well spent" (36). Charles Mignon in case study 6 reports using a similar journaling technique.

An alternative approach to documenting course enactment is to select and feature samples of work that are particularly key to the course design. Eli Passow, for instance, in case study 7, notes in his account of the rationale and design of Math 55 that collaborative learning is an important means for meeting his goals for student learning. Thus, his portfolio includes a section on collaborative learning, comprising problems he poses for student groups. Similarly, my portfolio includes selected artifacts and reflections related to the use of student writing groups, which are key to my conception of the course (and both common and problematic in the teaching of writing).

Other strategies and technologies for capturing the implementation of the course are listed in the box opposite. As suggested by the length of the list, the problem is not *finding* evidence but *selecting* it.

Documenting Student Learning

As noted in chapter 2, a defining feature of the course portfolio is its focus on student learning. Learning is, if you will, the conceptual centerpiece of the course portfolio as it has taken shape through the work of the AAHE Course Portfolio Working Group.

Deborah Langsam captures the view of the group when she notes, "Student voices lend credibility, interest, and life to a portfolio. Portfolios without evi-

---

Possible Evidence for Documenting Course Enactment

- videotaped class sessions
- peer observations of class sessions
- handouts that relate to key assignments
- audiotapes of out-of-class interactions (e.g., conferences with students)
- reports from student group work
- hard copy of electronic exchanges with individual students
- hard copy of class listserv conversations
- copies of lecture notes
- copies of overheads
- examinations and quizzes
- readings
- study guides . . .

How to Develop a Course Portfolio

Pat Hutchings, Senior Scholar, The Carnegie Foundation for the Advancement of Teaching

As noted in the introduction to this volume, and as illustrated in the case studies it contains, there is no single formula for a "good" course portfolio. What is "good" depends on purposes and context, on audience and occasion. Indeed, it is important to say at the outset of this "how-to" chapter that the course portfolio is still in the process of invention, still taking shape; even the name might turn out not to be quite what's needed (the AAHE Course Portfolio Working Group tried out several alternative terms: *course monograph, course investigation, course narrative*). What follows here is not, therefore, a recipe for course portfolio development but options for and ways of thinking about the kind of investigation and documentation that might contribute to effective teaching and learning.

Starting With Purpose

Lee Shulman comments in chapter 1 that the first question one often hears about course portfolios is, understandably, What goes in them? A more useful place to start is with the question of purpose.

Early on in its work, the Working Group identified three basic purposes a course portfolio might serve: personal growth, contribution to the field, and rewards. The nine cases in this volume illustrate how the choice of purpose drives other decisions about form and content.

Deborah Langsam, for instance, was primarily interested in personal growth. "I felt as though I was at a crossroads in my teaching career," she writes. "I have always enjoyed my teaching, have been excited by it, and have managed to do it fairly well (at least by the external measures of student evaluations and recognitions). But over the last few years I have become less comfortable with the lecture format that has been so central to the teaching of biology" (this volume, 57). Her portfolio thus becomes a vehicle for exploring possible transitions in her sense of herself as a teacher. Following from this purpose, Deborah's portfolio includes a high proportion of self-reflection (too much, she tells us, for one of her readers).

In contrast, Eli Passow wanted to use his portfolio to make a contribution to his field, by influencing other teachers of mathematics. Focusing on College Mathematics (Math 55), a controversial course in the department at Temple University, which is taught in two quite different ways, Eli uses his portfolio to argue for the more innovative approach that he and a group of colleagues embrace: "[T]he traditional course not only is inappropriate but, because it is so similar to ones that have troubled these students in the past, may actually be harmful" (this volume, 72). Not surprisingly, Eli's portfolio is front-loaded with a longer (relative to other elements in the portfolio) analysis of the rationale for his approach to Math 55.

Charles Mignon's portfolio was shaped in large part by an institutional decision-making context: "The time was simply right, for I faced a three-year post-tenure review and I thought the portfolio would serve to satisfy part of that institutional requirement" (this volume, 65). As a consequence, Charles was especially keen on keeping his portfolio as brief as possible; at 39 pages it was easily the shortest in the set developed by the Working Group members.

As illustrated by these examples, it is useful to begin the process of portfolio development by thinking about purpose, because purpose helps to sort out other choices. I might, for instance, put items in a portfolio intended for trusted friends and colleagues committed to my improvement that I might well *not* put in a portfolio aimed at future employers. But it should also be noted that although each member of the Working Group began by identifying a central purpose and audience for his or her portfolio, virtually all of us found that several purposes were actually served: Langsam notes that her self-reflective portfolio contains items that she could use as evidence in a personnel decision-making context like the one Charles Mignon faced. Charles, in turn, reports that the portfolio he prepared for a merit review also prompted considerable personal growth and learning. The traditional gospel of keeping improvement-oriented "formative" evaluation wholly separate from high-stakes "summative" evaluation might, it seems, be usefully drawn in less-absolute terms.

Finding an Organizing Principle

One of the possible pitfalls of both teaching portfolios and course portfolios is that laundry lists sometimes overwhelm larger purposes. "Too often . . . supporting documents dominate portfolio creation," one scholar of faculty portfolios observes; faculty focus on "a shopping list of possible portfolio items and determine which ones are most accessible. An emphasis on the 'what' rather than the 'why' may result in a superficial compilation of unrelated documents" (Millis 1995, 68). The antidote to this problem is to have a controlling idea, an organizing principle, around which the right materials can be selected, organized, and reflected upon.

Lee Shulman offers one way to think about an organizing principle in his four metaphors in chapter 1: course anatomy, natural history, course ecology, and the course as investigation. Additionally, members of the AAHE Course Portfolio Working Group found that having a focused question or hypothesis to explore made their portfolios easier to compile and more coherent to read.

William Cutler, for instance, organizes his portfolio around three themes that are central to a recent revision of a course he has taught for many years:

I do not teach History 67 the same way today that I did when I began my career in college teaching. In the early-1970s I organized my version of this course around the argument that American society changed from being communal to individualistic between 1600 and 1877. This approach seemed to work well then, and its underlying idea remains a part of my teaching. But after being away from this course for several years I decided that I needed to revise my version of it around a broader and less abstract framework that would more readily engage today's sophomores and freshmen. I chose freedom, diversity, and migration as themes because these concepts are at least familiar if not transparent to most Americans. (this volume, 22)

Thus, he tells us, "[the course portfolio for History 67] represents an attempt to demonstrate how I now use these three themes to make this basic course more accessible to beginning college students" (22).

Similarly, Donna Martsolf has a driving question she wants to answer in her portfolio on an advanced nursing theory course:

The typical graduate student, in my experience, enters a master's program in nursing with a way of knowing that is particularistic, tradition-based, and focused on "doing" and the "bottom line."

The purpose of Theoretical Basis of Nursing as I teach it is to help this student begin to think abstractly, conceptualize, question, and wonder how and why. I was, therefore, curious about how and when students made the transition from particularistic to abstract thinking. Each time I taught the course, it seemed apparent in final papers and presentations that the transition had occurred. However, I had no real knowledge about how that change transpired, and I wanted to use the portfolio to explore this question and make a case for my approach. (this volume, 26-27)

It is hard to overestimate the value of an organizing principle or question such as Donna's and William's. While a focus on a course is narrower than a focus on all teaching (as in a teaching portfolio), it is still the fact that no portfolio can represent the full and complete experience of even one course. Having a focusing question, a hypothesis, a puzzle, is key to the difficult process of selecting from the myriad evidence that could be included.

Components of the Portfolio

Three components are evident in the image of the course portfolio that shapes this volume. As noted in chapter 2, these three components follow from an analogy between teaching and a scholarly project, each of which entails *design, enactment,* and *results.* But how should each of these components be investigated and documented?

Documenting Course Design

Teaching begins not when students walk into the classroom but with earlier decisions about how to focus the subject matter of the course: what to include, what to omit, what goals for student learning are most important. Thus, it makes sense that the course portfolio begin with a section representing this process of design and planning. How to document this process? Probably the key artifact is the syllabus, and it's no accident that all members of the Working Group include a syllabus in their course portfolios. Because the syllabus might not speak fully for itself, however, each portfolio also includes reflective commentary on the syllabus. My portfolio, for instance, begins with a section on course design that includes a copy of the syllabus (five pages handed out the first evening, along with supplementary sheets for subsequent evenings, designed and distributed as the course unfolds), along with a four-page essay explaining why the syllabus looks the

dence of student work are not useful documents" (this volume, 62). And indeed, following this principle, virtually everyone in the Working Group found themselves gathering more information about student learning than we might in our "typical" teaching practice; because the course portfolio is so focused on learning, it virtually demands more (and more frequent) assessment of students. Donna Martsolf's experience is typical here:

> At the suggestion of the Working Group, I collected weekly feedback from the students about what they were learning, how that learning had occurred, and what difficulties they encountered in dealing with course content. This weekly feedback helped to illuminate my central question about how students move to a new, more abstract conception of the field. I included examples of all the students' responses at two points in the semester and one student's feedback every week. This revision added important evidence to the portfolio. (this volume, 27)

But this apparently straightforward principle — that portfolios need student voices and evidence of student learning — gets quickly complicated; representing student work poses conceptual and methodological questions. Orin Chein, for instance, reports that readers agreed that the early draft of his portfolio, which contained vast amounts of student work and "student voice," was "too bulky and that only a sampling of student work should be included. But how should that sampling be selected? Should it be the best work of the best students, or should it be selected from the whole spectrum of student performance? And how large a sample should be included?" (this volume, 41). Charles Mignon puzzles over the same point, noting that having read promotion, tenure, and merit files for many years — he "worried about how much student work to include, at what point in the narrative it would appear, and — more seriously — whether a single longitudinal sampling or a deeper vertical sampling would be more appropriate. Would it be more valuable to show the record of a single student's work from beginning to end, or to present all the students' responses to one exercise?" (this volume, 67).

These are hard and important questions, which have everything to do not only with what items should go into the portfolio but also with the kinds of claims (what Randy Bass calls in his case study "the burden of proof") that we can make about student learning and our power to "cause" or facilitate it. They are questions about the character and quality of evidence (which vary by field) and about the relationship between teaching and learning.

Because these questions of student learning are so central to this volume's conception of the course portfolio, chapter 5 by Daniel Bernstein is dedicated exclusively to them.

The Course Portfolio as Reflective Practice

Student learning is one measure of teaching effectiveness, but it is not sufficient. The course portfolio is a vehicle for embodying the idea that excellent teaching is teaching from which the teacher, too, learns; that is, teaching in which faculty do not simply undertake the tasks of teaching but undertake them as reflective practitioners interrogating their own practice and "going public" with their questions, findings, and new ideas. Once again an analogy to other scholarly work is apt. In the context of research, the excellent scholar is

"This section [on student learning] gets at a central feature of the course portfolio as a genre: the way it represents evidence about student learning, at least taking a stab at the question of teaching effectiveness in light of impact on student learning."
RANDY BASS (THIS VOLUME, 94)

one who not only completes and reports the experiment or the investigation but also comes as a result to new understandings of key issues as well as new questions to guide next stages of work (her or his own and the work of colleagues who build on that work). Similarly, to see teaching as scholarly work is to bring to bear an expectation of professional growth and learning.

This notion of reflective practice is a crucial component in all the course portfolios described in this volume. Eli Passow puts it this way:

> But more than anything else, a constant flow of reflective statements at the start of each section helps clarify for the reader the instructor's conception of the course. Why did I choose to give this particular assignment? Is there a reason why my tests are so long? Do the test results indicate that the students "got" the material? Without these reflective statements — what Working Group member Steve Dunbar (a mathematician from the University of Nebraska-Lincoln) has coined "the narrative glue" — the portfolio becomes simply a dumping ground for every piece of paper generated during the semester, and the reader comes away without a true feeling for the course. (this volume, 71)

How and where is this reflective aspect of the course portfolio embodied? One option is a longer reflective essay on the thinking behind the course; typically, such statements appear at the beginning of the portfolio, to set a context and framework for everything that follows. Many portfolio writers report that writing such a statement is especially useful in pulling the pieces together and examining long- and deeply held assumptions. But also useful are shorter reflective annotations attached to particular artifacts and materials — an essay attached to a syllabus, an evaluative summary of classroom assessment data, and so on. A third option is to dedicate a final section of the portfolio to the implications and lessons learned by the teacher. In general, the purpose of reflective components is to uncover one's "pedagogical thinking," and to answer questions about why various items are included and what they tell about one's teaching.

But How Much Is Enough?

The power of the portfolio comes from a process of selective sampling, rather than from amassing every possible scrap of evidence. Having an organizing principle or driving question helps determine which items are most relevant to the large argument of the portfolio. Charles Mignon notes that his "care in establishing the focus of the portfolio was particularly useful: Having a sense of what theme I wanted to illustrate helped me decide which student materials would be most germane as evidence" (this volume, 67).

But the question remains: How much is enough? Readers will not be surprised to know that the Working Group came to no clear consensus on this point. Eli Passow answers the question with a paradox:

> Axiom: An ideal portfolio is both brief and complete.
> Theorem: No ideal portfolio can exist.
> This tension between brevity and completeness is one that members of the Working Group have struggled with from the start. No reader wants to

wade through hundreds of pages in a portfolio — especially if he or she reads many portfolios, for, say, merit purposes. Though some of us have been more successful in trimming down our portfolios than others, there seems to be no easy answer to this problem. (this volume, 74)

The good news is that technology might provide a solution to this dilemma.

How Technology Can Help

As technology makes its way into classrooms and other instructional settings, it is also beginning to affect the development and use of teaching portfolios. For starters, technology makes the processes of teaching and learning public in a way they have not traditionally been (Batson and Bass 1996). Departmental homepages often include syllabi and materials from courses offered by program faculty; many faculty members are developing courses that are at least partly Web-based; exchanges between students and faculty, or among students, that were once private are now out there on course listservs and in chatrooms.

Randy Bass sees in these new technologies the necessary medium for documenting his teaching: "I have designed my course portfolio as an electronic, hypertext document primarily out of necessity: My teaching materials and my students' work are in electronic form, and therefore, only an electronic writing environment could adequately represent them" (this volume, 92). But he also sees in technology a solution to design problems faced by most faculty developing portfolios:

> *The hypertext format for a course portfolio also solves some problems that faculty authors of print course portfolios have encountered. Chief among these is the problem of evidence. How much evidence do you include for your readers? If too much, the portfolio is overwhelming; if too little, you run the risk of leaving readers with questions or skepticism. A hypertext format allows me to offer examples of evaluations or students learning in summary form and through representative samples, and then present readers with direct electronic access to the balance of evidence. Indeed, this is the format I have followed throughout.*
>
> *The choice of a hypertext environment for my course portfolio also gave me the luxury of multiple modes of organization and access.* (92)

Navigation Guides

Faculty developing course portfolios (and other new modes of representing teaching) should remember that readers need help making sense of new forms and genres. Deborah Langsam developed a number of strategies she believed would help readers make their way through her portfolio. But, she tells us, they wanted "still more" help (this volume, 61). What would assist them?

A first step is a clear table of contents, annotated perhaps, so readers can quickly see which items are likely to be of greatest interest. An executive summary, or some kind of overview/summary, also can assist readers to see the big picture before (or instead of ?) plunging into the details. Several members of the Working Group prefaced each section with a summary or overview.

Additionally, some members used tabs to divide major sections of the portfolio; a couple used color-coding to indicate which documents were of which kind (e.g., blue for reflective commentary, pink for student work samples, etc.).

Randy Bass's hypertext portfolio employs several "navigation guides," as he calls them, to assist the reader,

> *including a comprehensive index to course materials, related evaluation data, and the various sections of the course portfolio. Additionally, at the bottom of every page in the course portfolio is a "navigation bar" with each of the portfolio's components accessible through links.*
>
> *The "Portfolio Navigation Guide and Index" provides links to all of the online documents and pieces comprising the portfolio and the course.* (this volume, 96)

As noted in chapter 6, what is also needed in the way of aids and navigation guides is more information about how real readers read portfolios, as well as guidelines to focus and direct their reviews.

Working With Others

It's possible to imagine working in one's office, alone behind a closed door, to produce a fine portfolio. But working with others is clearly a source of added value. This was the experience of the Working Group members; Deborah Langsam notes the motivating aspect of working together: "I was stimulated to begin the process because I was part of a group of people who were interested in developing portfolios" (this volume, 58).

Some members of the group found ways to work with colleagues who were not in the group but who had special contributions to make. William Cutler involved two teaching assistants in his portfolio development process: "I asked each TA to keep a pedagogical diary, and these reflective statements offer an interesting and informative complement to my narrative and perhaps some reassurance that my narrative is not self-serving" (this volume, 21). Charles Mignon was especially vigilant about soliciting outside reader responses and then including them in his portfolio — a step he advises others to build into the process.

As course portfolios become more prevalent, campus-based centers for teaching and learning can play an important role in helping faculty find colleagues to work with — groups that might function on a local level more or less as the AAHE Course Portfolio Working Group functioned across campuses.

The Expense of Time

Virtually every faculty member or campus contemplating the use of course (or teaching) portfolios asks, How long does it take? Where will I find the time? Members of the Working Group have monitored the time commitment in order to answer these very reasonable questions — and not surprisingly their answers cover quite a range. A couple of members reported that the time commitment was 15 hours or less. Donna Martsolf estimated 20 hours for reflection and writing. At the upper end was Orin Chein, who tells us that he spent "in excess of 50 hours, and maybe even as many as 100" (this volume, 43). It is important, however, to note that many of his hours were spent on tasks that were useful not only for the portfolio but also for the teaching of the course. Chein counts

> *not only the time I spent writing introductory remarks and my reflective statement but also the time I spent expanding the syllabus, developing the study guides, creating and analyzing pre- and post-tests, developing discovery exercises, and doing the many rewrites that resulted from my evolving sense of what would make the portfolio (as well as the course) most effective. With one course portfolio now under my belt, I think I will be able to complete my second one (which I plan to do soon) in much less time — maybe as few as 20 hours.* (this volume, 43)

Ultimately, questions about time are questions about values, about what matters. When it comes to research, no one counts the hours; the work is assumed to be worth the time. Maybe spending 15, 20, even 50 hours a semester investigating and documenting one's teaching brings benefits sufficient to the cost.

A Course Portfolio for Midcareer Reflection

Deborah M. Langsam, Biology, University of North Carolina at Charlotte

There are four major reasons that led me to develop a course portfolio. For one thing, I felt as though I was at a crossroads in my teaching career. I have always enjoyed my teaching, have been excited by it, and have managed to do it fairly well (at least by the external measures of student evaluations and recognitions). But over the last few years I have become less comfortable with the lecture format that has been so central to the teaching of biology. In the first draft of my portfolio I wrote:

> It's . . . the type of teaching that works well for faculty who value content — and we do value content in our discipline. At the same time, we're not naive; we know that no one can stand and deliver the accumulated knowledge of biology. But we respond by carefully condensing material from texts, from the primary literature, and from our own research in our attempts to summarize the content of biology and make it more accessible to our students. It's not that we don't value "process," but rather we don't want it encroaching on our lecture time.

I am certainly not alone in questioning the value of delivering fact-laden lectures to students or in wrestling with the "coverage" dilemma in science courses. Currently, however, this is not a major conversation bubbling up in my own department. My conversations about these issues occur mostly with colleagues from other departments on campus or at other institutions.

I have experimented with strategies to engage students in large lecture classes (classroom assessment techniques, discussions, email, student portfolios), and I have tried to make the classroom a less anonymous place for the students. But this is uncharted territory for me; the new ways have often led to improvements, but they have not been coordinated into a complete picture of teaching and learning for a particular course, and they have not always worked. The course portfolio, therefore, was attractive to me because I saw it as an organizational framework for my thoughts about teaching and learning; it has become a laboratory notebook of sorts, providing a "space" where ideas, techniques, and assignments are conceived and then analyzed after their enactment.

My second reason is less connected to the question of, Why do a portfolio? and more to the question of, Why do a portfolio for a plant biology course? From a very pragmatic point of view, I chose to focus on a course that, at the time, presented me with the most challenges. The course is required for our freshman-level biology majors and has been taught for years in my department. But the course was new to me at the time I began my portfolio; a retirement in the Biology Department left a hole in the faculty rotation through the course, and I was tapped to fill it. In filling it, however, I was expected to carry on in the tradition of those who had developed the course, and that was the problem.

The course is a march through the plant kingdom, delivered lecture style to an audience of 180 to 200 students, who are often less than enthusiastic about having to take a botany course. As a newcomer to the course, I was not given the mandate — or the authority — to modify it in any substantive way. So while many course portfolios deal with the scholarly underpinnings of a course and the substance of what is being taught, I found myself using the portfolio to consider pedagogical strategies I might use to deliver course content that is departmentally determined. My goal was to discover and/or hone techniques that would stimulate student learning of this material.

A third reason for my interest in a course portfolio is related to a vision of my future development. I hoped that my portfolio could become a useful document for a promotion dossier. I did not write the portfolio to *be* that document. Instead, I saw the entries as the starting point; the entries that I developed might be modified and expanded over the next couple of years and could provide a menu of items from which I would pick and choose when I developed the dossier for promotion to full professor.

Finally, I was stimulated to begin the process because I was part of a group of people who were interested in developing portfolios. I had the support of colleagues, I felt a responsibility to contribute my share, and I had deadlines.

Getting Started

My initial attempt to construct a portfolio very much reflected the questions I was raising across the broad spectrum of my teaching. In fact, it would probably be hard to call that initial attempt a *course* portfolio, since it contained entries covering topics from a wide range of courses: the use of email in a nonmajor biology course, student reflections on the Plant Biology syllabus, and an analysis of student evaluations in an upper-division majors course. At the time, I wrote:

> I think of the material which follows as a "preamble portfolio." It's a type of development portfolio because it's not meant to be an official document circulated for evaluation and review. Rather, it's designed to help me sort through the teaching issues that currently concern me. So, I write it for myself and to share with a few trusted colleagues. And I write it with a purposefully broad focus. My experiments in teaching cross course boundaries and levels. The mistakes made in one class may influence my teaching strategies in another. The successes I enjoy in one course inform my choices for another course. As a result, a narrower spotlight seems premature. Instead, I am using this portfolio as a place to focus and articulate some of the ways that I am addressing my . . . teaching.

In retrospect, this was probably an essential step for me, given my agenda and the state of my knowledge about course portfolios, but I do not see it as a necessary step for others.

What did become clear, however, was that my scattershot approach made it difficult for colleagues to see the portfolio as an integrated document. They seemed intrigued by individual entries, but really could not place those entries into a unified picture of any one course or of my teaching as a whole. It was this feedback that led me to choose my Plant Biology course as the focus. Since it was a new preparation for me, I felt I had the most to gain there. Moreover, I was already engaged in thinking about issues of teaching and learning the course material. The portfolio seemed like an ideal way of organizing some of the planning, enactment, and outcomes of the course as they unfolded.

Selecting and Organizing Materials

A question faced by virtually everyone who decides to develop a portfolio is which materials to include. My first step in answering this question was to develop three criteria for the selection of entries:

1. Would the entry address a pressing issue or intriguing problem I was facing in my teaching?

2. Would the entry help me summarize or reflect on a new teaching strategy or technique that I might want to reprise, perhaps in a modified form, in a subsequent semester?

3. Were materials (artifacts) available that would bring student "voices" into the portfolio and provide evidence of student achievement, reflection, or evaluation?

Since the portfolio was essentially for my use, I felt no need to represent every aspect of my teaching. Undoubtedly, if I were to submit a course portfolio as part of a promotion dossier, I would look at the portfolio's balance to ensure that I had addressed a full range of teaching and learning issues. But at this juncture I was free to examine what most

intrigued me. The unifying feature of both my "preliminary" portfolio and the more focused portfolio dealing with Plant Biology was a framing statement I developed to place the specific issues I was addressing within the larger context of my teaching philosophy and practice.

Issues in the Development and Design of the Portfolio

As is true for most faculty, time was an issue for me. The AAHE Course Portfolio Working Group provided my "excuse" for developing the portfolio. Here was an opportunity to put theory into practice and to have a group of colleagues respond to that attempt. I had a good bit of experience with teaching portfolios, and I have often required my students to keep portfolios. So the genre did not seem at all foreign to me; I thought of it as an extension of a reflective dossier.

But there is no doubt that this was an add-on activity for me and that carving out the time to think about the portfolio, to gather and sort through materials, and then to reflect on them was a challenge. I found myself bumping up against deadlines (reasonable as they were) because I spent eight to 12 hours per entry. I should note that others I have spoken to have found the process less time-consuming. Suffice it to say I am not a speedy drafter.

Another issue involved the question of "audience." For whom was the portfolio being written? If, in fact, the portfolio was being developed for me — to help me rethink how, what, and why I teach the way I do, then a tight organization should not be necessary; I should have been free to consider the issues that I found compelling, to package them loosely in whatever form I chose, and to make the connections that seemed most useful to me. Would I really need to "document" what I had done or to articulate my thinking in a written form? And if I did, how much background information should be provided? The course and departmental context were certainly obvious to me, so why bother writing about them? And yet, why bother developing a portfolio if I were its only audience? I could certainly *think* about my teaching without assembling documents or reflecting in writing. But the point of the portfolio is to engage others in conversations about teaching that might be helpful to my continued development as a teacher. Even formatively, I needed to think about outside readers, who they would be and whether they were familiar with the particular circumstances of my teaching.

Finally, the issue of "length" concerned me. I was fairly comfortable with limiting the number of entries in the portfolio and highlighting a subset of teaching issues and strategies. But within those entries, how much documentation was enough? In one entry, for example, I discussed an assignment that asks students to address a number of questions related to their examination of the course syllabus. The inclusion of student work was extremely important, to illustrate not only how I respond to students but also how the assignment ultimately benefits them.

But I found myself asking, How many samples of student work (or instructor-generated materials) are sufficient? Should samples be selected randomly? Should samples reflect all levels of student work? or reflect the percentage of students exceeding, meeting, or failing to meet expectations? A selective file of supporting documentation is likely to raise questions of whether the samples provid-

ed are biased to reflect a particular agenda. A complete file could overwhelm a potential reviewer. This is not an issue I feel I have resolved.

Benefits of the Portfolio Development Process

First, I was reminded, once again, that writing is a learning tool. Committing my thoughts to paper helps to clarify them and prevents me from skipping past the "hard parts" (i.e., the places where my thinking is muddy). To explain to others is to explain to myself.

Second, thinking about the portfolio stimulated me to be proactive. The commitment to writing a portfolio not only kept me thinking about my course; it also kept me thinking about my *teaching* — as I prepared to teach the course and while the course unfolded. By doing the portfolio I found myself in the position of being a witness to my own classroom practice in a way I had not been before. In particular, it was the portfolio that kept me thinking about my goals for student learning and about ways that I could prove to myself and to others that I was helping students meet those goals. It made new approaches to old problems in the classroom less likely to evaporate into the land of good intentions. As I wrote in my portfolio,

Too many times, my good ideas about teaching are lost because they pass through my brain as fleeting thoughts or as unwritten resolutions to "do better." The opposite is also true. I repeat mistakes or make do with old strategies because I have not taken the time to rethink my game plan for a lesson or activity. My sense is that the very act of capturing those fleeting thoughts, of formalizing the game plan, of facing the failures, and of underlining the successes will help me move to new places with my teaching.

Third, I have come to appreciate that the coherent approach provided by the course portfolio can help me avoid the pitfalls of temporarily placing new assignments and strategies — like so many pedagogical band-aids — on the problem spots of a particular course.

Finally, the portfolio process mirrored the process of teaching. I came to a point in my portfolio where I stopped but did not feel I was finished. It was a logical place to stop, but I could see that there was more that could follow: classroom research to assess student understanding/accomplishment, new iterations to improve existing assignments, updated material to be incorporated. Neither a portfolio nor the course that it describes can be "done" as long as the course is being taught. There is always something new to incorporate, reconsider, readjust.

Learning From Portfolio Readers and Reviewers

In many ways, the reviews of the portfolio were encouraging. And a number of trends were evident. For the most part, reviewers understood the developmental nature of the portfolio and seemed to value the potential benefits of the process to the individual instructor and to the overall improvement of instruction. As one reviewer noted, "I really do find value in the reflective nature of course portfolios. At a minimum, they provide a springboard from which faculty can engage in meaningful discussion about a specific course."

And the "springboard" effect was evident; a colleague who teaches the required freshman-level Animal Biology course wanted to show the portfolio to other colleagues involved in teaching Animal Biology. Her goal was to persuade them to adopt some of the pedagogical strategies that were illustrated in the portfolio. Also interesting were colleagues' requests to borrow the portfolio in order to illustrate, particularly for junior faculty, the types of entries that might be developed for a course portfolio.

Having said all this, I hasten to add that a minority opinion came from one reviewer who encouraged me to "reduce the parts that deal with your own process."

The reviews also reinforced the importance of having an organizational framework for the portfolio. For the most part, reviewers seemed to be able to navigate through the entries with relative ease: "The fact that you divided it up with the tabs made it easier to reference different sections and gave me a feeling of breaking it up into bite-sized pieces," one reader reported. The dividends of organizing (table of contents, tabbing, color-coding, introduction) far outweigh the busywork of attending to these details. Even with these measures, however, some reviewers ask for still more organization: "You could improve access to the portfolio by making it clearer to the reader where the 'meat' lies. Your accompanying letter made it clear that you thought the 'meat' was in the clear tabs, but this is not conveyed in the Table of Contents."

Not surprisingly, reviewers were most engaged by the parts of the portfolio that included student work. One reviewer stated, "Student responses in the form of portfolio entries and specific midterm narratives gave the reader a more complete picture of the student population and motivation in the course. This was particularly helpful and provided the usually missing information about students that most peer observers would not get." Another found the student voices "compelling." Overall, the most valued student entries were those that showed student learning and progress. And reviewers were most eager to see samples of work that illustrated a *full range* of student achievement (exceeding, meeting, falling short of expectations).

The value of portfolios, and mine in particular, for purposes beyond personal development was less clear to reviewers. By and large, reviewers seemed to feel that portfolios could have a place in high-stakes decision making. But — and I agree with this — none viewed my explicitly developmental portfolio as the proper document for submission. Reviewers expressed concerns about the time involved in portfolio development and evaluation. And they were wary of embracing portfolios in the personnel process until useful criteria were established for their preparation and review.

At least one reviewer raised the issue of faculty integrity: "If one is making a case for tenure/promotion based on excellence in teaching, these portfolios may be good — but how much is it possible to manipulate what's in them by a less-than-honest person who is just trying to impress the review committee?"

Overall Lessons and Reflections

1. Never underestimate the value of organization. By their very nature (since they contain personal reflections, course artifacts, and student work), portfolios can be daunting documents to read. Anything that helps to organize portfolios for the reader is, by definition, a good thing.

2. Student voices lend credibility, interest, and life to a portfolio. Portfolios without evidence of student work are not useful documents. Portfolios without samples illustrating a range of student work are suspect.

3. There's always a tension between giving readers full access to potentially helpful information and keeping portfolios manageable. Web-based portfolios are, no doubt, one way to ensure that interested readers can easily link to a fuller range of work samples.

4. The entries I have found most interesting are those that illustrate problems and challenges in teaching. The pristine "wasn't I wonderful" portfolio is boring. My fear is that if and when portfolios are used for summative evaluations, vulnerable faculty will feel the need to produce these self-promotional documents, and the usefulness of the portfolios will be negligible.

5. Much of what I learned was learned from the reviewers of my portfolio.

A Final Quandary

In 18 years of teaching, I have never been asked to make the type of systematic analysis of my classroom practice and teaching philosophy that the course portfolio allowed — and even forced. I have done some of it, independently, in bits and pieces while developing a new course or wrestling with a particularly challenging problem in pedagogy, but nothing as sustained or intensive as my portfolio. I cannot help wondering why we do not demand this of ourselves and of our colleagues.

At the same time, I must report one more reaction from a reader of my course portfolio, who (albeit in a minority opinion) questioned whether portfolios were a suitable vehicle for the purpose I chose: "My own bias is that a portfolio is not the most efficient way to go about personal development. Portfolios are directed outward. Development is a (primarily) inward process. Keeping a journal of ideas about your teaching might be a more efficient way of promoting your own development."

I will end this case, then, by admitting that this comment struck a chord, for I think the point is well taken. In reality, perhaps, the "purely developmental" portfolio that I assembled was not really purely developmental. I was part of a group studying portfolios (thus, I was pursuing a scholarship of teaching and was motivated by the social benefits, intellectual challenges, and responsibilities of being a group member); I may be submitting a promotion dossier in the near future (the portfolio was a foundation for documenting teaching effectiveness); and post-tenure review is on the horizon at my institution (the portfolio could be evidence of scholarly activity and teaching effectiveness).

Would I, given most faculty loads, recommend a portfolio to someone who was strictly interested in instructional development and had absolutely no other plans to use or disseminate it? Perhaps not. It is an intriguing thought.

Post-Tenure Review: A Case Study of a Course Portfolio Within a Personnel File

Charles W. Mignon, English, University of Nebraska-Lincoln

Three factors figured into my decision to develop a course portfolio. First, I found the idea helpful because of the changing nature of my field. The canon of American literature has changed substantially over time, and a number of what Paul Lauter in the *Heath Anthology of American Literature, Vol. 2* (1990) calls "lost, forgotten, or suppressed literary texts" have emerged from the newly discovered richness and diversity of our culture: "In the 1970s a whole new scholarship developed that examined the cultural implications of gender, race, and class for our understanding and appreciation of literature" (xxx).

In trying to rethink for myself the courses I teach in American literature, I felt the need to describe their foundations and implicit designs more fully, both to myself and to my students. I wanted to see whether I could demonstrate that I was continuing to develop as a professional in the classroom in ways that made sense in light of developments in my discipline. Indeed, the crisis in the discipline became the challenge that my portfolio would take up.

But the second reason I found the idea of a course portfolio helpful to my teaching is that I felt I had to find ways to connect my teaching more directly to these new developments in the shifting nature of my discipline and, more broadly, to research in teaching and learning. It seemed a course portfolio might help me forge and explore these connections in ways that would be accessible to my peers as intellectual property. In short, I wanted to do what Lee Shulman has talked about: make my teaching "community property."

Third and finally, my decision to prepare a portfolio was taken in the context of a personnel review — a "summative" review, that is, even though much of the work on my portfolio was accomplished in a spirit of "formative," improvement-oriented collaboration with others. The time was simply right, for I faced a three-year, post-tenure review, and I thought the portfolio would serve to satisfy part of that institutional requirement.

A Conception of Effective Teaching

I have come to see the formative process related to teaching as entailing the following steps: (1) identifying and addressing issues raised in a former iteration of a course; (2) inventing possible solutions to face problems; (3) revising course materials as a result of reflection on these points; and (4) recording the results of the next teaching of the course to assess the revisions.

I believe that these formative adjustments, informed by deliberate reflection on teaching and learning and undertaken in the light of current research in classroom assessment, are the *sine qua non* of effective teaching and demonstrate one of the qualities of a scholar-teacher: perseverance, the mind continuing to inquire. Thinking I had made improvements in my teaching, I wanted to test this assumption by constructing a course portfolio to see whether the case I might make was convincing. So, although my portfolio was initially keyed to a required post-tenure review, I was silently motivated by a curiosity as to whether I could document my sense that students had learned from my work in organizing classroom activities. I also wanted to make a scholarly argument, in the sense that my preparations were grounded in the discipline of English and the course itself was placed within developments in the field.

Establishing a Focus for the Portfolio

I began my portfolio by consulting colleagues in the AAHE Course Portfolio Working Group, receiving particular help from Deborah Langsam (Biology, University of North Carolina at Charlotte), who addressed the specific focus of the university-required file, for that would determine the choice of materials for my portfolio and set out the rhetorical problems I wanted to address within it. After consulting with Deborah, I decided to focus the portfolio on a fairly general topic: continuing to develop as a professional in the classroom, a topic of special interest to me at this point in my career (I am a tenured, full professor with 35 years of experience and within five years of retirement).

In an opening section of the portfolio (entitled "Focus"), I describe the thinking behind this choice:

> The rationale is the continuation of my development as a

professional in the classroom, development which includes innovation. Senior faculty members can draw upon their past experiences, upon research on teaching and student learning, as well as upon advice from their colleagues when they start new projects, and they can in this light take risks in their teaching that others might not be willing to take.

This first step — establishing a focus — was crucial to the unity, coherence, and development of the portfolio, and I recommend care and deliberation at this early phase of the work.

Next, I had to decide how, specifically, I would tackle this theme of professional development. My solution was to build my file around three courses — one of which would get the full "course portfolio" treatment to illustrate this theme. For Introduction to English Studies (English 200), I would concentrate on student outcomes; for Diversity in Early American Literature (English 432/832, the focus of the more full-blown course portfolio), I would emphasize active learning; for 20th-Century Fiction (English 205), I would treat the issue of closing a course. Descriptions of the course content and the student audiences for each of these courses appear in the appendix to the file.

Collecting and Assembling Evidence

In the early spring of 1996, I began the process of collecting and selecting appropriate materials. I deliberately started 10 months before the whole file was due (January 1997) because I knew that would enable me to arrange small sections of time throughout the year to gradually build up the file.

There are several ways of describing this process. In one sense it resembles a cycle of learning: exploration, invention, and application. In terms of the parallel between teaching and research, a course portfolio, like a monograph, involves goals, implementation, results, and meaning. And, as a product, a course portfolio has parts appropriate to its various purposes. In still another sense, the course portfolio reveals in its own underlying design the necessary reflection on the purposes of a course, the means by which these purposes might be realized, the student learning to be encouraged, and the means of assessing the results.

Representing the Student Experience

The process of developing the portfolio necessarily involved the collection not only of course materials (course description and schedule, class exercises and handouts, exams, and so forth) but also the students' work (journals, papers, and exams), which I used for evidence to confirm or rule out the presence of learning. (I needed the students' permission to use their work for my classroom research, so I adopted a form that one of my colleagues in the Working Group had invented, and invited the students to sign the release of their work for this purpose.) This is where the prior care in establishing the focus of the portfolio was particularly useful: Having a sense of what theme I wanted to illustrate helped me decide which student materials would be most germane as evidence, because I wanted the students to see these materials in a certain way.

Reflection and Connection

The next step in the process was to prepare reflective memos on the materials: short, connecting narratives to explain features of course design such as underlying principles, the making of the schedule, and the character of assessment. Then, with the various sections complete, I needed to provide short framing pieces. These included an initial overview, a table of contents, the "Focus" section mentioned above, and sections on pedagogy and curricular context.

Peer Review and Revision

The final steps in the process were review and revision: I needed peer review of the portfolio and time to make the necessary revisions. One colleague suggested, for instance, that I add a retrospective memo to explain the changes I would make in the course for its next iteration. This provided a welcome closure to the commentary on this course.

Problems and Puzzles

One problem I faced in the above process entailed the selection of student work for evidence. Because I was committed to brevity in the construction of the portfolio (having read promotion, tenure, and merit files on and off for many years), I worried about how much student work to include, at what point in the narrative it would appear, and — more seriously — whether a single longitudinal sampling or a deeper vertical sampling would be more appropriate. Would it be more valuable to show the record of a single student's work from beginning to end, or to present all the students' responses to one exercise?

I later realized that these questions are best answered in light of the particular purposes of the course and what I wished to illustrate about it. For example, in English 432/832, my purpose was to document active learning on the students' part. For this purpose, a vertical sampling would seem appropriate, so I collected responses from all my students to a portion of one of my teaching journal entries. (These materials appear in the portfolio's appendix.) Additionally, the "learning letters" I requested from them would become part of the "student voice" in my portfolio.

A second problem worth mentioning was Time's devouring hand. Here my principal problem was in the scheduling of my completed file for external review. I would like to have included readers' assessments of the portfolio as part of the documentation submitted for departmental review. But by the time I had completed a campus review and revision, I had not enough time to send the material out for external review. My solution to this problem would be to revise the schedule to allow for this important additional step. I would recommend at least 12 months for the whole process, with two months for external review, which, though currently an extraordinary expectation, may become, at some future point, common practice, as it is in the review of research. That is, just as professors and chairs currently negotiate a list of external reviewers to assess research, the same procedure will, I believe, come to be adopted for the external review of teaching. Course portfolios will be important in focusing the external reviewer on those features of teaching that the faculty member wishes to stress, giving greater control over the framing of the file to the teacher.

Readers' Reactions

Though time constraints prevented me from including readers' reviews in the file that went forward to the personnel committee, I did have a chance to solicit reviews — all very helpful — from three readers at a later date. I learned from them, first, that it is important to be clear about the roles that readers intend to take. For example, in beginning his response to my portfolio, Professor Larry Andrews (English, Kent State University) described the three perspectives he would bring to bear, as "(a) peer mentor, . . . (b) hypothetical peer evaluator, . . . and (c) project colleague." Similarly, Professor Richard Turner (English, Indiana University Purdue University Indianapolis) described his role as follows:

> My task [is] fourfold: (1) to understand Professor Mignon's achievements in three courses based upon the materials he has sent, (2) to evaluate the work in terms . . . of current practice in the field, (3) to offer to this review process the perspective of another teacher of English, and (4) to offer to Professor Mignon any suggestions about his practice which might occur to me during the review.

I conclude from these two examples that a first rule for assessing portfolios is that the reader be clear about the purpose and scope of the review and any specific criteria that will be used to judge success.

The second thing I learned from my readers was that there were gaps or absences in the presentation of my material. Professor Turner suggested an addition: "Of specific help would be some capsule explanation of the expectations and requirements the department or the university sets for its students such as might be found in university planning documents and mission statements." This is especially pertinent to the larger curricular context, and since I believe that teachers will increasingly need to justify their courses more clearly in relation to departmental and college mission statements, I intend to introduce such connections more directly into a section on curricular context in any future portfolio I construct. Professor Andrews pointed out a lack of depth in my reflection on student responses to English 432/832: He rightly saw that the students' negative rating on course goals could have been "engaged a bit more, perhaps, in the reflection conclusion." The questions he posed for me in that section of the review showed me that there was much more to be considered in the students' evaluations of the course.

I draw a second rule for reading portfolios from these examples: that readers should note ways the course could be improved.

The third thing I learned from readers was that the portfolio needed a clearer articulation of what I think English Studies is about and what I want students to be able to do or know at the end of the course. Dr. Kathleen Quinlan (Education, Australian National University) showed me that my "background probe" for the English 200 course seemed to assume only the most basic level of understanding: She wrote, "If I were to borrow from Bloom's taxonomy of educational objectives for a moment, the background knowledge probe gives the impression that you are primarily concerned with knowledge or comprehension, which Bloom says is the lowest level of understanding." In the context of the purpose of this course — to give students the opportunity to write and think critically about literature — the probe in itself was insufficient to test the learning I was looking for. Quinlan's advice was penetrating: "Develop a background knowledge probe that is more in line with the types of things you expect students to learn."

Professor Quinlan's assessment of the portfolio as a whole fell into the category of advice helpful to revising classroom practices; she was candid in suggesting sources for me to consider as a better way to understand different classroom cultures, different styles of interacting, and new (for me) rubrics for thinking about student learning.

The fourth thing I learned from my readers was that whatever the format used, my reviewers responded with seriousness, intelligence, and relevant detail. The tone of these assessments was one of scholarly and critical distance. Thus, a final rule might call for professional distance, objectivity, and candor from readers — the same qualities we expect in the review of our scholarly work of other types.

How the Portfolio Changed My Practice

What most surprised me was how the portfolio increased my sense of unrealized potential in the classroom. I began to see teaching and learning in a more scholarly way — comprising a body of knowledge much in the way one's "discipline" does. Becoming more aware of this body of knowledge, I began to read selectively in the research literature on teaching and learning, discovering new ideas and strategies for use in the classroom that made me much more aware of the cognitive atmosphere in my classes. I saw — increasingly — many more opportunities to apply principles of good practice in my classes. This does not mean that I am yet resourceful enough in these practices to take immediate advantage of specific situations, but I have become more aware of opportunities for new applications of these principles.

Lessons Learned

My best advice for colleagues in English considering whether or not to undertake a course portfolio comes in three related suggestions: worry, be skeptical, and leave yourself open to the possible benefits.

You should worry about three things: (1) how your assigned courses relate to your department's, college's, and university's missions; (2) how your course design and course materials reflect your own commitment to these missions; and (3) how your course materials and teaching practices relate to student learning. These "worries" actually represent professional responsibilities, and the course portfolio is an occasion to address them in a meaningful way.

Skepticism is appropriate in thinking about the costs and benefits of developing a portfolio. What are the drawbacks (e.g., the element of time) and the obstacles to be overcome (e.g., gathering materials, writing reflective memos about course design and classroom practices)?

Why would one decide to develop a portfolio? Perhaps one is dissatisfied with the reliance on student evaluations as the sole measure of teaching effectiveness; perhaps one sees a day approaching when students will demand more attention to results in their courses; perhaps the discussion of a new learning paradigm and its emphasis on the quality of learning is challenging; or perhaps one simply wishes to learn more about classroom assessment techniques or pedagogical content knowledge. Whether the motive is formative or summative, the gains must outweigh the drawbacks.

Finally, one should remain open to benefits. I hope that this case study reveals some of the benefits that were most important to me in my first foray into the course portfolio.

A Portfolio That Makes a Point

Eli Passow, Mathematics, Temple University

In 1994, I attended the initial meeting of participants in AAHE's national Peer Review of Teaching project; our aim was to work together over the next several years to develop means of documenting effective teaching beyond the usual student evaluations. What became clear to me (and to a number of others whose work is represented in this volume) was that course portfolios can serve as a major component of that documentation. As a consequence I became a member of the AAHE Course Portfolio Working Group, which was charged with refining the nascent ideas that had emerged at that first meeting in 1994.

The Idea of the Course Portfolio

The purpose of the course portfolio is to provide a series of snapshots that, together, give a reasonable sense of what went on during the semester in a selected course. The portfolio should begin with some background: who the students are, how the course fits into the curriculum, some of the problems in teaching the course, and what the goals are. It should contain a syllabus, accompanied by a reflective statement meant to elaborate on the choices made by the instructor in the design of the course. Assignments, handouts, examinations, and student work are major pieces of the necessary evidence. Student evaluations should also be included, but they appear to be more useful in narrative form than in the usual computer-scored one. A self-assessment by the instructor is also valuable.

But more than anything else, a constant flow of reflective statements at the start of each section helps clarify for the reader the instructor's conception of the course. Why did I choose to give this particular assignment? Is there a reason why my tests are so long? Do the test results indicate that the students "got" the material? Without these reflective statements — what Working Group member Steve Dunbar (a mathematician from the University of Nebraska-Lincoln) has coined "the narrative glue" — the portfolio becomes simply a dumping ground for every piece of paper generated during the semester, and the reader comes away without a true feeling for the course.

Portfolios have many possible purposes. While the primary one may be evaluation of an instructor's effectiveness, a portfolio also has a reflective purpose. It is important to stress that a course portfolio need not be a static document. In fact, it is most useful when compiled over a period of years, as it can then document the changes that have taken place from year to year. The updating of the portfolio gives the instructor the opportunity to reflect on what has worked and what has not, and how best to correct and improve the course.

Another use of the portfolio is argumentative. Some courses are controversial, with several approaches possible. The portfolio enables the instructor to argue his position by showing how effective his particular approach has been in the classroom. You can make a case for a certain set of readings or for particular nonstandard assignments. If you believe strongly in collaborative learning, you can use the portfolio to demonstrate that the students have learned things through this approach that would not have been possible with conventional lecturing.

A Portfolio That Makes a Point

My own portfolio is of this last, argumentative type. It originates in a long-standing discussion that has taken place in our department over the nature of a core curriculum mathematics course for students in the humanities, arts, and other disciplines that do not require *any* mathematics for their majors. About 10 years ago, Temple University introduced a core curriculum, which includes a mathematics component. Students whose disciplines demand specific subjects, such as calculus or business mathematics, take those courses. Everyone else takes College Mathematics (Math 55), which is intended for a very general audience, including students from humanities, the social sciences, art, music, education, social work, and so forth, a total of more than 2,000 students per year. (The social science majors are the only ones who are required to take any additional mathematics — statistics.)

These students have often had negative experiences with mathematics, and they enter this course with great trepidation and low expectations. Like many people, they fear and dislike mathematics, yet, paradoxically, they *overly* respect the authority they feel is conveyed by numbers and formulas. They are unlikely to challenge anything an instructor tells them, never having developed the ability to think critically in mathematics, which they view

as a meaningless subject. Given these perceptions, is it any wonder that as many as one-third of them fail to complete the course on their first try?

The Debate About Math 55

So what is appropriate subject matter for students such as these? This question has been debated fiercely in our department for many years, and, in fact, we run two Math 55 courses. Some instructors (still a majority) advocate a traditional course, emphasizing algebraic skills and manipulations, a formula-and-procedure approach many students find vaguely familiar. The traditionalists argue that students should become comfortable with equations and graphing, maintaining that the essence of the field lies in the computations, which they see as "doing mathematics."

My feeling, one shared by many colleagues, is that since few of these students will use mathematics in their discipline, we have an essentially free hand. I prefer that students achieve understanding, rather than just learning procedures. In fact, some of us believe that the traditional course not only is inappropriate but, because it is so similar to ones that have troubled these students in the past, may actually be harmful. A more innovative approach is needed.

At about the same time that our core curriculum was introduced, a text that was revolutionary in both content and style was published. Beginning with realistic problems that arise in many different contexts, *For All Practical Purposes (FAPP)* then develops the mathematics necessary to solve them. Many of the topics are nontraditional, and some are not to be found in any text intended for freshmen. However, the exposition is on a level consistent with the limited mathematical skills of the students. Shunning jargon, and utilizing a minimum of notation, the authors manage to convey a sense of the overwhelming breadth of mathematical applications.

I began using *FAPP* as soon as it appeared and have taught the course from this text many times. It is now available as an option to all Math 55 instructors, and about one-third of them choose it. The book helps me achieve one of my most important goals: to change the overwhelmingly negative attitude toward mathematics that many of the students bring to the subject, an attitude that propagates from one generation to the next. To overcome the national disaster that threatens us in mathematical education, we must break the cycle somewhere, and this terminal course is our last opportunity to reach these students.

Lifelong Learning

If the skills that have been emphasized in traditional math courses are inappropriate to our audience, then what should replace them? We come to a second goal of the course, as I see it, which is to impart *lifelong* skills, ones that these students can use on a daily basis. To accomplish this, I find it necessary to make use of supplementary sources, since it is difficult to convince students that they will find much of relevance to them in the text. The best auxiliary is a good newspaper. It is familiar and accessible to the students, and they trust it — perhaps too much! And yet, there are many articles and issues that bewilder them.

Take polls, for example. How is it possible to obtain highly accurate estimates when polling just 1,500 out of 100 million voters? How are the Nielsen TV ratings obtained? Or medical testing: What's a control group? a placebo? Why is it that one study shows that Vitamin E can protect against cancer, while another makes it seem ineffective? Which one should we believe? In education: How do we measure the success or failure of the new standards for the teaching of mathematics in elementary and high schools?

Since many of these issues involve public policy, one of the goals is to produce better-informed citizens, who are capable of understanding mathematical and statistical arguments, thereby improving their ability to make intelligent decisions, at least at the ballot box.

To reach these goals, I require the students to read the *New York Times* and other papers and magazines regularly. Their main assignment for the semester is to collect a set of articles from the print media that involve statistics. Students are then required to analyze these articles for their statistical content, focusing on how thorough the reporting is. My experience has been that many students benefit substantially from this assignment. Some have commented that they previously avoided reading any article that contained numbers, but that they were now confident enough to distinguish between specious arguments and solid ones. (Whether they really have developed this ability or not is not clear; more important is that their *attitude* toward mathematics often improves.)

The Portfolio

My portfolio includes a couple of sample statistical scrapbooks, since one of my main aims is to show what the students are capable of accomplishing. I also include copies of my exams, which are also unconventional. Rather than merely testing the students' ability to perform computations, the exams are conceptual in nature, involving higher-level thinking. It is not unusual for a question to require a mini-essay as an answer, rather than just a calculation. Also, I might give the students a brief article from a newspaper and ask them to analyze it. While the students may initially be unfamiliar with this approach to testing, they do become comfortable with it after several weeks.

As I said earlier, students are more likely to respect sources outside their textbook. To exploit these feelings, I distribute a large variety of articles taken from the media and secondary sources. Some are intended to serve as models of the type the students will use in their statistics project, while others deal with related issues. One article that I use regularly is about the 1954 field test of the Salk polio vaccine. This article is a wonderful summary of all of the concepts that we study about medical testing but, because it involves a real-life situation, has much more of an impact on the students than the theoretical descriptions that are found in the text. I include copies of these articles and handouts in my portfolio.

The portfolio also represents my attempt to incorporate a good deal of collaborative learning in class. I frequently introduce a topic by posing a problem, which I ask the students to grapple with in small groups. I then ask them to report on their thinking. Remarkably often, the students come close to solving even difficult problems, although they may have not had any previous exposure to the topic. However, even if they fail to solve the problem, their efforts are valuable, since the investment of their energies makes them more interested in the solution than if they had heard a polished lecture from

me. I include the problems that I have posed in the portfolio.

Representing Student Learning

My colleagues and I in the AAHE Course Portfolio Working Group have become convinced that the student voice is vital in conveying a full picture of the conduct of the course. Hence, I include in my portfolio selected samples of my students' work: the statistical project mentioned earlier and selected tests and papers representing a range of student performance. Additionally, if the class is sufficiently small, I include complete student evaluations. I do not rely on the standardized, computerized evaluations, because I have found that my own forms, which require the students to answer in prose, are much more valuable to me. Since these evaluations are three or four pages long, I cannot include all of them if the class is large, so in this case I choose some representative ones. This problem leads to the following result:

> *Axiom:* An ideal portfolio is
> both brief and complete.
> *Theorem:* No ideal portfolio
> can exist.

This tension between brevity and completeness is one that members of the Working Group have struggled with from the start. No reader wants to wade through hundreds of pages in a portfolio — especially if he or she reads many portfolios, for, say, merit purposes. Though some of us have been more successful in trimming down our portfolios than others, there seems to be no easy answer to this problem. One possibility is to summarize certain sections, such as the student evaluations, and place the "evidence" in appendices.

Costs and Benefits

How long does it take to construct a portfolio? I have not kept a log, but I do not believe the process was very time-consuming. Much of the work involved activities directly related to the conduct of the course. The introductory material on the background of the students and the rationale for my approach probably took more time than anything else, but I had given this course a great deal of thought over the years, and I had written significant sections of that material in preparation for the first meeting of the Peer Review of Teaching project mentioned at the beginning of this case study. (If I were to assemble a portfolio for a new course — especially one I have not taught before — this part would take a good deal of time.)

Collecting the assignments, exams, and readings takes no time at all. Looking at the portfolio in retrospect and summarizing the results of the semester might take a few hours, but this is one of the main benefits, because the review process is helpful in subsequent years.

My work on course portfolios has affected my teaching significantly. Since I am constantly evaluating the effectiveness of the material and approaches that I use, I am much more conscious of what works and what does not. Hence, I refine the good, reject the bad, and introduce fresh material more regularly than in the past, which helps improve the course from year to year.

For example, in the past I asked the students to keep a journal in which they were to monitor their progress in the course, their feelings about it, or anything else they chose. However, it became clear to me through the evaluations that few students benefited from this assignment and some even resented it. (Perhaps I was at fault here. Since our classes are quite large, I read the journals only occasionally, so that the students received sporadic commentary from me.) As a result, I have dropped this assignment.

In another direction, a few of my colleagues have used my portfolio and find that it gives them new ideas for assignments, approaches, and testing. In fact, this might be one of the major benefits of portfolios, since they enable instructors to exchange ideas about their courses. I look forward to seeing some of my colleagues' portfolios, in the hope that they will be equally useful to me.

Putting the Focus on Student Learning

CHAPTER

5

Daniel Bernstein, Professor of Psychology, University of Nebraska-Lincoln

There are many activities that faculty members can engage in to develop their teaching. Attending workshops on teaching techniques, videotaping classes, and consulting with specialists are all useful ways to work on teaching; many faculty also find that there are benefits derived from the creation of a teaching portfolio. Given this array of options, one might ask, What is distinctive about the course portfolio as one among many development activities? This volume answers that question in a variety of ways and voices. My argument in *this* chapter is that the major benefit of the course portfolio lies in uncovering how effectively the course goals for student learning are being met. In what follows, I will discuss the importance of this focus on student learning, as well as the issues and challenges this focus raises for those developing course portfolios.

An Interaction Between Teaching and Learning

The lens of the teaching portfolio focuses nicely on the teacher. By contrast, a course portfolio is a wide-angle lens that includes learner performance as well as teacher performance, and the relation between them is at the center of the picture. In this wide-angle view of optimal teaching, learners acquire deeper understanding as a result of teaching, and teaching practices evolve as a function of their success in generating understanding. The distinctive focus of the course portfolio is in revealing how teacher practice and student performance are connected with each other.

A focus on the interaction of performance and results is not unique to teaching; it is also characteristic of the documentation of research and professional outreach. In a research article or consultant's report, one would rarely find an account of the scholar's work without a description of its results, and the report would certainly claim a connection between the activity and those results. Moreover, excellence in the domains of research and applied scholarship is characterized by flexibility and adaptability in matching performance to intended outcomes. A skillful researcher might, that is, adjust her or his approach on the basis of preliminary results; a consultant who does not at first obtain satisfactory results in a service setting makes adjustments so as to achieve the desired outcome. And so it is with excellent teaching: If learners are not reaching a deep understanding of the material, the teacher makes adjustments in order to more fully meet course goals. Indeed, such a transactional relation is a benchmark of excellence in scholarly practice.

The Assessment Imperative

In work on my own campus and beyond, I find many faculty today who concur that good teaching is about this "transactional relation" to learning. Where things get difficult is in their knowing whether and how deeply students are actually understanding course material and reaching course goals — which is where assessment comes in.

77

On the one hand, assessment is familiar ground to faculty; all of us gather evidence about student learning and evaluate that evidence in order to provide feedback — and to give grades. On the other hand, new, sometimes daunting models for assessment have been increasingly in the air in the past decade. There are now a number of national and regional conferences, growing examples of campus practice, and an impressive array of literature that readers can turn to (see for instance, Angelo and Cross 1993; McMillan 1988; Walvoord and Anderson 1998; Wiggins 1998; Wiske 1998), some of it proposing quite radical departures from the kinds of assessment that faculty have traditionally engaged in. Proponents of "authentic assessment" argue, for instance, that the traditional course examination is a rarified form of human behavior; that there are very few real-life situations in which a person is called upon to work alone and without access to source materials to produce a written answer to an abstract hypothetical question within a specified and usually brief timeframe. Critics of traditional assessment (e.g., Perkins 1992; Wiske 1998) suggest that learning and understanding should be measured by putting students into appropriate and complex situations requiring them to collaborate with other people, integrate knowledge and critical skills from several specific domains, analyze competing contextual constraints, and put a workable plan into effect. This vision of assessment has a clear and intuitive appeal for many teachers; we recognize that it would be terrific if learners who have read our assignments, done our problems, and listened to our analyses actually brought those inputs together in a productive way when called upon to do so. But of course all of this is easier said than done.

In short, not all faculty are ready to jump with both feet into all the latest models of assessment. But the literature on assessment, and its evolving practice, has much to teach those of us attempting to develop course portfolios. Indeed, the benefit of the course portfolio is not that it transforms one into an education specialist but that it makes visible the need for and power of information about student learning.

Building Assessment Into the Course Portfolio

As Pat Hutchings noted in chapter 4, one of the puzzling elements for most faculty developing a portfolio is how to represent student learning; that is, how to build in the process of assessment. The four suggestions that follow derive both from the general literature on assessment (as noted above) and from the experience of faculty who have actually developed course portfolios:

Focus on the match between assessment and course goals. While it may seem obvious, assessment should focus on the kinds of learning the course aims to produce. Many a faculty member has discovered after the fact that poor student performance likely resulted from teaching to one kind of understanding while expecting learners to produce a different kind. I had a colleague who was very proud that he never asked on a test anything that he had explicitly taught in the class. He could give a very articulate explanation of the importance of generalized understandings, and the need for students to use ideas and tools in new contexts beyond what has been taught. Unfortunately, his course did not have any planned strategy for promoting those generalized skills in students.

"I wanted to hold my own feet to the fire, using the portfolio to look much more closely at whether and how my decisions about course design and conduct actually contributed to student learning."

PAT HUTCHINGS
(THIS VOLUME, 85)

My colleague was also proud that few of his students earned top grades; very few learners in his course acquired those conceptual skills he so lovingly measured. A course portfolio would have placed this circumstance — a mismatch between ambition and result — in the foreground, leading to a consideration of the relation among goals (well articulated), measures (appropriate to the goal of generalization), and methods of instruction (not directed toward abstract skills).

To put it differently, the course portfolio is a kind of self-discipline that can prompt faculty to examine the all-important relation of the skills intended, the skills being taught, and the skills that are ultimately assessed.

Use existing assessment data whenever possible. Many faculty upon first encountering "student outcomes assessment," whether in the context of a mandate from an accrediting association or the development of a course portfolio, assume that what is needed is something wholly new and different, something they do not already do or know how to do. In fact, as pointed out above, all faculty assess student work, and the generation of a course portfolio can be made a less daunting task if the evidence of student learning comes from activities that take place as a regular part of the course. The grading of examinations and other assignments is, for example, an important form of assessment, and a course portfolio would certainly include examples and summary data from those existing measures of student understanding. Reflection on the evidence might, admittedly, involve some new time, but gathering evidence about student learning should be a regular process of conducting the course.

At the same time, readers may be struck, as I am, by the case studies included in this volume, virtually all of which report that the decision to undertake a course portfolio brought with it an awareness that more and better evidence about student learning was needed. Thus, while "existing evidence" is good grist for a course portfolio, many faculty developing one find themselves exploring new assessment strategies that can give a richer picture of student learning.

Include a variety of kinds of evidence. There are many ways that faculty learn how much of the course material students understand. While the formal assessment (course examinations, major papers, projects, etc.) that goes into the records of a course is certainly important, a course portfolio can also take advantage of "trace materials" from other assessments that are used in a primarily diagnostic or formative way. As documented by Angelo and Cross (1993), classroom assessment strategies can give instructors an image of student understanding without their scheduling examinations or grading homework assignments. The "minute paper" is perhaps the best-known example; students are asked in class to write anonymous, brief (i.e., "minute") statements of what they do or do not understand about topics in the course, giving the instructor a read on their grasp of key ideas before the next meeting. A class journal can also serve this purpose. A faculty member I recently talked with described her use of a "dialogic journal," which she keeps in an accessible place in the classroom and in which she and members of the class write regularly about how things are going, why, what changes might be useful, and so forth. Similar information could be gleaned from a Web-based chatroom that can be accessed continuously by students and teacher alike. Yet another source of useful feedback is the "Small Group Instructional Diagnosis," in which I would invite a colleague to my class (I meanwhile would leave) to lead the students through a series of questions about how the class is going (Braskamp and Ory 1994). All of these informal, and quite simple, low-stakes assessments can provide material for a course portfolio. Indeed, a number of the portfolios described in this volume include such information as an important part of their picture of the student learning experience.

Be purposeful about selecting evidence about student learning. In case study 4, Orin Chein reports on his efforts to prune the voluminous amount of student work he included in the first draft of his portfolio. He puzzles over how much to include, and how to select an appropriate and credible subset of the fuller collection. He is of course correct that there is no reason to include in a course portfolio all the student performance that takes place in a class; doing so only overwhelms the reader. And he is also correct that actual samples of student performance are a key element of the course portfolio.

Fortunately, there are several strategies for selecting examples of student performance. On my campus, for instance, we are piloting a strategy whereby faculty identify randomly on the first day of class a manageable number of students (for example, seven or 10) whose work is then collected and tracked throughout the semester. The idea is to create an archive of specific examples (work that is graded and commented upon) that can be used to investigate and illustrate changes in student understanding during the semester. In combination with a grade roster that shows the distribution of performances for *all* students, this sample gives rich meaning to the range of student understanding in the course. It also allows an in-depth study of the evolution of individual students' work as they progress through the course. The longitudinal development of individual understanding is a window into teaching and learning that might well find a place in a course portfolio; indeed, Pat Hutchings's portfolio contains one longitudinal case study of this type.

An alternative to tracking individual students over time is to select completed work on key assignments and assessments. This might mean selecting "benchmark performances," displaying the best work achieved as an index of the potential quality of the experience. It might mean selecting a range of work: two excellent, two average, two unsatisfactory. Readers can then get a sense of the teacher's goals and standards.

The main point here is that readers do not need (and probably cannot bear) to see all of the work done in a course, and the course portfolio is a means for the instructor to organize levels of learner understanding and make them apparent to readers of the portfolio. As in other forms of scholarly writing, the presenter gives a full representation of ideas without asking readers to repeat all of the observations that led to the conclusion.

The Substance of Assessment: What Learning Do We Care About?

The four suggestions above speak primarily to issues of process; my aim is to address questions that faculty routinely ask when trying to represent student learning as part of a course portfolio. But what many faculty also want guidance with is the *substance* of assessment: What should be assessed? What knowledge and skills are most important? This chapter is not the place to lay the question to rest. Indeed, there is no universally accepted, standard set of outcomes, and it would be inappropriate to treat any of the models found in the teaching literature as sacred text, with faculty striving to assess only at the highest level or trying to include every category in an author's index of skills. What can be said, however, is that it is important to *assess a range of skills*, and not only those that are simplest for us to measure or easiest for students to master. And it might, therefore, be helpful to lay out a sort of typology of skills and learning.

Relatively Concrete Material

Most courses introduce learners to a variety of new information — vocabulary, facts, intellectual conventions common to the field, procedures essential to its conduct, and so forth. When I teach about the acquisition of language in a course about learning, I want students to know what Chomsky means by "language organ." Faculty teaching poetry want students to know that a sonnet has 14 lines. In a chemistry class, students need to learn the basic safety protocols for conducting a lab. Though the teaching of facts has rightly been taken to task in some circles, the grasp of relatively concrete material is part of what it means to know the field. Thus, it is entirely appropriate that the assessment included in a course (and documented in a course portfolio) include measures of students' facility with this kind of information — which is, after all, the raw material of the field.

Application and Comparison

Most faculty, teaching most courses, also value a number of skills in a medium range of conceptual difficulty. These include, for instance, the ability to make relationships among ideas or observations; assessments at this level might ask students to "compare and contrast" two love sonnets, or two phenomena related to language acquisition. Another approach is through questions that ask for application of a procedure or analytical tool in a new context. Students might be asked how ideas or tools apply to newly provided raw material; they might be asked which of the many analytic tools previously learned is most useful to a new context. The main difference from the more concrete level is that the students use ideas in some way, demonstrating a more active intellectual role that goes beyond recognition of a term or idea.

Synthesis and Evaluation

At the advanced level of understanding in any field we might look for some form of new or evaluative use of ideas by a learner. Here faculty might ask students to combine ideas and raw material that were presented separately, working to find some conclusion that can only be drawn when the two are considered together. Synthesis of this kind is a form of scholarship highly valued in many disciplines, and recognizing connections among observations and phenomena is a source of intellectual creativity. Another form of advanced understanding involves the evaluation of alternative perspectives or arguments. If they understand the conventions of evidence or analysis in a field, learners should be able to explain how they would evaluate which of several alternative positions provides the best account of some of the raw material in a field. Like application, this is a form of using the tools of a discipline, but it is a more complex form in that multiple options are available to be analyzed and considered.

Learning as a Test of Teaching

This chapter — and indeed much of this volume — argues that questions about the effectiveness of teaching cannot be answered without reference to learning; that learning is, if you will, the test of teaching. I endorse this formulation, but I would like to conclude by saying a bit about the realities of its enactment — be it through course portfolios or some other vehicle.

In this, I am reminded of a section of Randy Bass's portfolio entitled "Learning: A Narrative Analysis." It is, he says, his "stab at the question of teaching effectiveness in light of impact on student learning." He reviews a number of examples of student online projects, citing evidence that course goals have been met in some cases, while in others uncovering "lingering concerns." But in a related section, entitled "The Burden of Proof," he also enters an important caveat:

> *I found myself asking a larger question regarding the burden of proof on any single course to demonstrate learning outcomes, let alone a course working with new tools and approaches that are not to be found elsewhere in a curriculum. Most of what we expect from any given course is contextualized by the recurrence of those same skills or approaches in other courses. Ideally, any major curriculum is characterized by certain common methods and conceptual tools across a course of study. . . . [W]hile there are some things that I can do [to promote student learning] one truism will remain: An anomalous course in the curriculum will always be limited in its impact. By this, I simply mean that what can be accomplished in one course is completely different from what could be accomplished if students were encountering some of these skills across several courses.* (this volume, 95)

Bass's point is a crucial one for those of us interested in course portfolios and other new ways of representing teaching and learning (and especially where such documentation will be used for personnel decisions). Though we might well want to emphasize the importance of impact on student learning, it is impossible for any individual instructor to claim sole responsibility for the learning that takes place during his or her course. Educational settings simply do not allow for the sort of experimental method that would enable us to make such claims. And of course we all know that student effort, prior preparation, and the simple passage of time have a good deal to do with student growth in our classes — more, sometimes, than our teaching per se.

On the other hand, the course portfolio can put a focus on student learning in a more modest but very powerful way. While one might not claim that the teaching of the course is the exclusive cause of student learning, a portfolio can help faculty show where the course experience *contributed* to student growth.

This case is often best made by a longitudinal account, showing how learners' understanding changed over the unfolding of the course and showing those forms of identified good teaching practice that were included during that time. For example, one might document the evolution of a learner's understanding by alternating samples of performance with samples of the feedback given and instruction offered. The sequence of events documented gives a plausible account of the growth of understanding.

One might also use evidence of learning to identify a trajectory of performance. If a clear benchmark of quality student learning is identified, an instructor might measure learner understanding against that benchmark in successive semesters, noting that each successive class is moving progressively closer to it. Evidence of such a trajectory of class performance across offerings would be strong support for improvement on the teacher's part.

In this sense, the course portfolio model, with its focus on student learning as feedback to help instructors develop their teaching methods, is completely congruent with the framework in *Scholarship Assessed*, in which teaching is considered a form of scholarly work in which excellence is gauged in part — not exclusively — by looking at results in terms of understandings achieved by students. Excellent teaching is, by this measure, a process of ongoing, purposeful reflection on the relation between teaching practice and learner success. It is this process that the course portfolio is distinctly able to capture.

A Course Portfolio for a Creative Writing Course

Pat Hutchings, English, University of Wyoming

My interest in course portfolios began many years ago, actually, with student portfolios, which, as a teacher of writing, I have often asked students to develop as a way of representing and reflecting on their work and learning during the semester. From there to the idea of a portfolio representing the teacher's work — my work — was an easy step. Moreover, since I have in recent years taught only one course at a time (as an adjunct professor), the idea of a portfolio focused on a single course seemed made-to-order for my circumstances. Thus, when the opportunity arose to work with a group of faculty developing course portfolios as part of AAHE's Peer Review of Teaching project, I jumped at the chance.

Original Hopes and Purposes

I was particularly interested in two benefits that I thought might be forthcoming from a course portfolio. First, the course portfolio seemed to provide an occasion for colleagueship about teaching and learning that I lacked. As an adjunct faculty member (first at the University of Maryland and then at the University of Wyoming), I found myself dashing to class to teach my creative writing course, then dashing back to my "other life" as a staff member at AAHE (and now, the Carnegie Foundation for the Advancement of Teaching). I had virtually no conversation or engagement with other faculty in the program. The course portfolio, and particularly the experience of developing the portfolio as part of a working group of faculty from around the country, seemed a route to meaningful exchange.

Second, I was motivated by the same principle that shaped the "prototype" course portfolio developed by professor William Cerbin (see chapter 2) — what he called "learner-centered evaluation." That is, I wanted to hold my own feet to the fire, using the portfolio to look much more closely at whether and how my decisions about course design and conduct actually contributed to student learning . . . and what *kinds* of learning. I wanted to know whether my students were doing more than going through the motions of trying out various poetic forms; whether they were learning, as my syllabus says, "to approach writing as a process of deliberate choice making and problem solving." I wanted to know whether the multiple drafts I required were actually helping them to see that revision is intrinsic to good writing — not a punishment or a final spell-check and spiffing up (as many students see it) but an occasion for fundamental rethinking and reshaping, and part of the fun of working with language.

It was with these two hopes in mind that I began developing the course portfolio described below. Both have been fulfilled.

The Course and Its Students

My portfolio focuses on Creative

Writing-Poetry (English 2080), an elective course for the English Department at the University of Wyoming, where I am a visiting professor. The course is pitched primarily to sophomore English majors and minors. However, the actual student enrollment is much more diverse than that description suggests. In the semester I taught the course, I had three first-year students, five sophomores, one junior, and four seniors; in addition, the class included one graduate student and one faculty member (who was auditing the course). Of these students, only three were English majors or minors. One young man was a devotee of Allen Ginsberg; one young woman was a serious reader of Anne Sexton and Sylvia Plath. But for most of the group, the level of knowledge about poetry as a tradition and a craft was extremely modest.

On the other hand, in a short written survey of interests and goals that I asked students to complete the first night of class (we met on Wednesdays at 7:00-9:00), about half the group reported that they were currently writing or had previously written some poetry, and almost to a person they reported that their interest in the course was in finding new ways to express themselves, to unleash their creativity, to find outlets for a self that felt cramped in a curriculum of computer science or engineering (or whatever).

My "Take" on the Course

This profile of students — as relative beginners with little formal knowledge of poetry and with a strong impulse to "be creative" — is in my experience very typical for creative writing courses in an undergraduate curriculum. It is also the basis for my "take" on the course represented in

my portfolio. In a first section of the portfolio, on course design, I write:

Lee Shulman has proposed that we think of our courses as scholarly arguments, and the metaphor certainly pertains in the case of my poetry writing course. I do indeed have a view of the field — an argument about it — that I hope to have students share by the end of the semester: I want them to understand the experience of writing as a way of constructing and shaping the world, of making meaning, and, importantly, of making that meaning accessible to others.

This last point is the real trick in this course, since the term "creative writing" . . . conjures up for my students a scary but cathartic gush of personal feeling, self-expression, emotion not "recollected in tranquility" but spewed forth with no test of success but that "it's true" and/or deeply felt. . . . Let me hasten to say that . . . like the students, I feel a need for creative self-expression; however, I shape the course around a somewhat different idea, that though writing does indeed entail strongly felt personal thoughts and feelings (let us hope so), it is a process that entails deliberate choices, careful revision, and constant testing against the responses of real readers.

This is a point of view that I make clear in my portfolio but that I share very explicitly with students, as well. The syllabus (which as noted above is in the portfolio) says:

The term "creative writing" implies, perhaps, a more per-

sonal, self-expressive use of language than that of technical reports or cookbooks or newspapers. But if you're writing only for yourself, if you think of creative writing mainly as therapy, this course is probably not what you're after. Writers hoping to sharpen their work need readers who will honestly, thoughtfully, thoroughly respond to that work. I don't mean judging whether it's good or bad, but saying how it "works on them" — how it tastes, smells, what mood it conveys, what jumps out, what fades into the distance, what lingers and haunts. . . .

My explanation and exploration of this organizing principle of the course — writing as a process of problem solving and choice making — is, in my view, the most important section of the portfolio (comprising the syllabus itself and a four-page reflective essay about it). It's important because before I forced myself to explain myself in this extended way I did not fully understand my own theory of the course. It's important, too, because it gives the reader a context for making sense of and evaluating the three sections that follow.

The Unfolding of the Course

The second section of the portfolio focuses on *the session-by-session unfolding of the course,* as reflected in four assignments and lines of activity. This was the hardest section to assemble, because there was so much to choose from. Should I feature the fun way I have students introduce themselves at the beginning of the semester so that a sense of community begins to develop? Should I discuss the visits by guest

poets? Both are, to my mind, valuable uses of class time, but I rejected them and many other possibilities in favor of four things that seemed to me more clearly related to the organizing principle (choice making, problem solving) of the course. These include a series of assignments aimed at helping students develop criteria for "poems that work," the use of student groups for peer critique and feedback, activities designed to help students transfer learning about poetry writing to other kinds of writing, and the student portfolio (submitted twice in the semester) as a vehicle for self-reflection and integration.

In retrospect, I think I might usefully have added (or substituted) one additional activity: my individual conferences with students in which we talk at length about one or two poems that they have selected for inclusion in their portfolio. As noted later in this case, one of the readers of my portfolio inferred from it that I had little interest in the personal aspects of my students' writing, in the feelings and ideas they were striving to communicate. I think I might have mitigated that (mistaken) sense that I'm a relentless, cold-blooded formalist by some account of individual conferences, which are in fact often very personal, very much about "substance," very much about what my students "go through" in the writing process.

Documenting Student Learning (and My Own)

Which brings me to the third section of the portfolio, focused on *what students learn.* This is tricky business in any course, but especially so in a course where learning is distinctly nonlinear (students may write their worst poem last) and where virtually every required piece of work is open-ended, with no "right answers." As I wrote in the portfolio, in this context it seemed important "to look at the teaching-learning connection from different angles, and with different evidence in view." Thus, I included (1) a longitudinal case study of a single student's progress through the course; (2) a range of final student work (i.e., from the end-of-semester portfolio) from two A students, one B student, and one C student; and (3) data sets from periodic, anonymous classroom assessment from all students. Numerous samples of student work are included in this section, all with student permission.

Additionally, I prefaced the entire section with a more synthetic account of what the evidence tells me about student learning. I note, for instance,

> *Students — most of them — make real progress in the way they think about and practice (or report that they practice) the writing process. Many begin the course dead set against revision, especially of poetry, which they believe leaps full-formed from their hearts; most end the course at least claiming [in the reflective essay in their final portfolio, for instance] to see the value of revision informed by responses from diverse readers.*

But I also note:

> *Most students make less progress (than indicated in the previous observation) as poets. While almost everyone writes one or two quite respectable poems, poems to be proud of, they don't move ahead in some neatly linear fashion. This, in my view, is not a failure of the course (or students) but a circumstance of the way we all*

> *learn as writers. It's a loopy, cyclical process, with a lot of starting over, not a neatly developmental one.*

I confess that it was the development of the portfolio — the self-discipline and reflection required by the process — that brought me to these realizations, which were probably down there somewhere in my pedagogical subconscious but had never been so consciously acknowledged and therefore understood.

Not surprisingly, then, I also included a final section in my portfolio focused on *my own learning and reflection*. This is the place where I try to pull together a number of realizations that are noted in this case — about the rationale for my choices, about ways to make various aspects of the course more fully congruent and mutually reinforcing, about new insights about my students' learning. I also included several observations about the portfolio itself as a tool for reflection and improvement.

The Portfolio Development Process

One question always asked about portfolios — certainly it is asked of me when I present my portfolio to groups — is, How long did it take? It's important, I think, to parse that question in terms of a larger one about what I did and when.

During the semester I was teaching the course, I spent very little time on the portfolio per se: The things I was doing for the portfolio I would have done anyway. These included, for instance, the use of classroom assessment strategies that would give me an evolving sense of how the course was going, what was working and what needed attention or revision. I *did* spend a bit of extra time copying student work so that I would have a good pool of samples to draw on when I got to the actual selection process. I also took 10 minutes of class time later in the semester to explain to students that I was developing a portfolio and that their work would be an important part of it. I made up a permission form and asked students to sign if they would not object to having samples of their work included — anonymously, of course. Everyone signed and, interestingly, insisted that their names be included: They wanted their work identified; they were proud of it!

At the end of the semester, I sat down to put the pieces together and create what I hoped would be a coherent document. This was a sort of "one fell swoop" process, which took me between 12 and 15 hours over the course of a week. The first and (I now see) key task in this process was to write the reflective memo about the syllabus, a four-page document that really sets the stage for everything that follows and that provides the framework for my later decisions about what to include and why. That is, the portfolio turns on my account of the rationale for the course design; everything else follows from that.

Readers' Responses to the Portfolio

In the past year, I have shared the portfolio with various readers — members of the AAHE Course Portfolio Working Group and then several readers who were external to our process. While their reactions (which I requested in writing) vary in the details, a number of themes emerge.

First, my readers all reported finding the portfolio interesting and engaging. One wrote, "it invited me in — invited me to write a response to you — to engage with you in a dialogue about both pedagogy and poetry." Another reported that my account of making assumptions about the course explicit in the syllabus was intriguing to him and an idea he intended to incorporate into his syllabi in the future. It is of course possible that my readers were simply being polite, but they seemed actually to find the reading interesting.

Readers also agreed that the inclusion of (and reflection upon) samples of student learning was an essential center of gravity for the portfolio. One noted,

> *After reading your portfolio, I am even more convinced of how important it is to include samples of student work (with some range of performance, as you did) as well as the feedback provided by the instructor. [I included work with my comments on it, and also my longer, typed responses to student portfolios.] The feedback spoke volumes about how much attention you were giving individual learning of each student . . . in relation to course goals.*

Another said that my treatment of students' experiences and learning was "exemplary. I got sketches of individual people in the class, as well as a broad overview of the entire class and their response to the course." A third confessed to wanting even more in this regard: "I needed a better sense of who these students were."

All of my readers were able to imagine ways that the portfolio could and should be used, citing its power to prompt self-reflection (from me); its potential as "a tool for analysis in a 'teaching circle,' or even a more-structured workshop or seminar for new or experienced faculty." One imagined that a department might be able to use a portfolio like mine for purposes of program review. Very interestingly, however, the reader whose substantive expertise (the teaching of writing) is closest to mine confessed that the portfolio "suggests how the [course] design works — but not necessarily *how well* it works. With no changes, the portfolio would be useful for a number of purposes. . . . But *if* I wanted to make some assessment about the effectiveness of your teaching, I would need more or different materials." In particular, she wanted a more in-depth, fine-grained account of how my work with individual students contributed to their learning.

With this in mind, I might, in a future iteration of the portfolio, do a more in-depth case study of one teaching/learning episode, rather than trying to cover four different aspects of the unfolding of the course.

Finally, and most distressingly, one reader noted that the final impression left by the portfolio was of a teacher who taught poetry as craft, showing little concern for the substance of student writing or, indeed, of poetry itself. This is not, I think, an accurate description of my approach, but in my attempt to present my teaching around a coherent intellectual conception (writing as problem solving) I edited out, as it were, aspects of my teaching that are more personal, more serendipitous, more human, perhaps.

Toward a More Scholarly Discourse About Teaching

I mentioned at the beginning of this case that in turning to the course portfolio I was looking for a vehicle for professional exchange about teaching and (especially) about student learning. I would end this case study by noting that this is a need felt by many faculty. Some, like me, are adjuncts without a ready group of colleagues. Many are full-time faculty with colleagues all around but whose culture provides no real opportunities for what Parker Palmer calls "good talk about good teaching"; the conversations that *do* take place are typically ad hoc, in passing in an elevator or corridor, often in the form of student bashing or nostalgic recollection of better days. Even more-sustained conversations have a hard time getting beyond the exchange of personal anecdote (be it woeful or victorious).

What most strikes me about the course portfolio is that it provides a different way of representing teaching — a way that is, though still personal, still particular and story-like in many instances, also scholarly. For me, the key to this shift is the possibility provided by the portfolio of framing issues not as purely personal (my problems and successes in the classroom) but as "problematics" that are *inherent* in the teaching of the subject area. For me, the course portfolio is an attempt to "construct" teaching as an intellectual project rather than as an exclusively personal performance.

A Hypertext Portfolio for an Experimental American Literature Course

Randy Bass, English, Georgetown University

The course portfolio is a relatively new genre that is being developed to enable teachers to discuss both the scholarly and the pedagogical dimensions of their teaching; it provides a reflective outlet for articulating the intentions and experiences involved with teaching particular courses at a given time in a person's career. This case focuses on a hypertext portfolio I developed for American Literary Traditions, a course that I first taught in the spring of 1997, and again in fall 1997.

A Mix of Purposes

I chose to write a portfolio for American Literary Traditions (ENGL 210) because I created the course with the intention of testing a set of assumptions about new approaches to teaching an introductory American literature course. Specifically, I wanted to introduce new technologies into a mainstream, introductory American literature course setting, and I wanted to see if these technologies, in combination with other pedagogies and methods, could successfully support an approach to American fiction that emphasized the complexities of literary and narrative form, but in a way very accessible to students who were new to the subject. Writing the course portfolio on American Literary Traditions has given me an opportunity to reflect seriously on two semesters of experimentation both in the context of my own professional development and as a contribution to the field of teaching American literature.

First and foremost, I have written the portfolio as a way of being rigorous with myself in trying to track, document, and interpret the kinds of student learning that are taking place in my courses. In 1995, when I first taught in a networked computer environment, with a workshop pedagogy, I encountered many problems and the lowest student evaluations (by a wide margin) of my teaching career.

Given that this was the year before my tenure review, I considered this drop in student evaluations very dangerous. Even at that time, most of my professional energy was being spent on the use of new technologies in teaching culture and history. Everything was at stake in making new approaches to teaching with technology work in my home setting at Georgetown. Consequently, I welcomed the opportunity to write a portfolio, because it allowed me to formalize the experimental and hypothetical stance with which I approached my teaching and to be systematically reflective about it.

Second, I have written a course portfolio as a formal part of my tenure dossier. As with many faculty, teaching is a highly integrative activity for me, a site for crossing boundaries between scholarship and pedagogy. Especially because I work with new technologies, and frequently

91

show this work in presentations, my course materials and student work are particularly public (as is the work of most faculty teaching their courses with online components). My teaching is not only a contribution to my local context but also a public and portable contribution to my field. A course portfolio enables me to reflect on my teaching in a research model and in a publication format so that it might be subject to peer review, and part of a professional conversation, as would any other part of my dossier.

Choosing a Hypertext Environment

I have designed my course portfolio as an electronic, hypertext document primarily out of necessity: My teaching materials and my students' work are in electronic form, and therefore, only an electronic writing environment could adequately represent them.

The hypertext format for a course portfolio also solves some problems that faculty authors of print course portfolios have encountered. Chief among these is the problem of evidence. How much evidence do you include for your readers? If too much, the portfolio is overwhelming; if too little, you run the risk of leaving readers with questions or skepticism. A hypertext format allows me to offer examples of evaluations or students' learning in summary form and through representative samples, and then present readers with direct electronic access to the balance of evidence. Indeed, this is the format I have followed throughout.

The choice of a hypertext environment for my course portfolio also gave me the luxury of multiple modes of organization and access. For example, the first section, enti-

tled "Contexts," discusses the personal, institutional, and disciplinary contexts for American Literary Traditions. Most notably, perhaps, I discuss that my use of technology in a mainstream literature course at Georgetown makes it relatively anomalous in the curriculum. I have been teaching with technology for several years, experiencing both the positive and less-than-positive sides. In creating this course, I have drawn on these experiences, as well as on several areas of the discipline related to the teaching of narrative and teaching with technology.

Also in the "Contexts" section, I point to some other cohort courses on the Web with related interests in hypertext and narrative form. Writing a reflective course portfolio, then, especially one in electronic (hypertext) form, allowed me to situate the course in multiple contexts simultaneously.

The portfolio is divided into four main sections, in addition to an executive summary and cover letter (which includes much of what appears here at the beginning of this case).

Capturing Pedagogical Intentions

The longest section is entitled "Argument," in which I lay out my pedagogical intentions for the course overall, the course design that I felt would facilitate those intentions, and a summary of claims that I make about what appears to work well and still need revision in these approaches. Readers who click on "Intentions" (within the "Argument" section) will find an account of how I hoped to help students improve their understanding of American narrative, articulated as five different learning goals:

1. *To broaden students' paradigms of narrative form.* I want students to walk away from this course with a more complex notion of how narrative functions than they had when they came in. I hope that means that they will acquire new ways of reading and writing that lead them to see narrative as the complex intersection of form and meaning. They tend to come in prepared to learn about categories, themes, and techniques. I am more interested, however, in their development of a broadened "paradigm" of understanding about fiction and narrative in general.

2. *To get students to see narrative fiction as functioning with "complexity" and as a system of meaning that has an internal coherence as well as multiple discourse contexts.* Students by and large come in with a tendency to read novels transparently, or simply as portrayals of human experience and emotion. Although I don't want them to lose this human dimension, I do want them to think about narrative fiction in several new ways: to see narrative fiction as a "system" with its own apparent coherence; to see literary language as different from nonliterary language in that it is a discourse defined by overdetermination and excess of meaning; and to see literary narrative as a discourse (both intentionally and unintentionally) in multiple registers of meaning.

3. *To engage students with the World Wide Web and hypertext tools both as a resource and as a metaphor.* If the goal of complexity implies getting students to see narrative fiction as functioning something like a system of meaning, then a counterpart goal was getting students to see literary texts as existing in a field of other texts. In this vein, I was hoping that the Web could be used not only as a resource for research but also as a metaphor for seeing literature as a constructed object and a coherent structure with multiple contexts. It is my goal in an introductory literature course to work toward this through active processes, trying to create combinations of reading and writing experiences whereby most of the students — not just the best ones — come to understand literature as a constructed object, as both a coherent structure and a text situated in multiple rhetorical contexts.

4. *To help students "slow down" their experience of reading and writing — to "defamiliarize" (to use a Russian formalist term) the reading and writing process.* Defamiliarizing, or dehabituating, the reading and writing process means asking students to think about continuities between their reading of literature and their writing, to see their own interpretations as constructions in the same way that literature is a construction. One of the ideas I wanted to test with a constructivist approach was that nontraditional writing environments, and electronic tools, could be used to create contexts in which that process of close reading and argument building was made inevitable through assignments that asked students to re-create their readings within constructed hypertext projects.

5. *To open up student notions of American literature as being constituted by multiple traditions and a history of playfulness with narrative form.* First and foremost, I wanted to create an introductory course that was not a survey but an introduction to the idea of American literature. In this sense, an introduction to American literature carries these connotations for me: to think about literary traditions in American literature as having thematic as well as formal dimensions and to think about "America" as a referent for American literary expression in a way that comes from multiple traditions and expresses itself, in part, through the complexities of form and meaning described above. By calling the course "American Literary Traditions" I hoped to not only foreground the plurality of influences but also encourage students to think of traditions as dynamic rather than static categories.

Capturing the Conduct of the Course

The third section of the portfolio is the annotated syllabus (another uniquely electronic feature), in which the course syllabus is annotated with reflections about several key moments of the course, accessible in "pop-up" windows where the syllabus and the reflection are on the screen simultaneously. A central thrust of this section is to uncover the ways my students pursue the above five goals through a week-by-week, unit-by-unit reflection on the syllabus. Here I reflect on how students, by working both inward and outward with literary texts, using traditional classroom and networked classroom settings, work toward each of the learning goals.

The annotated syllabus provides the main narrative of the portfolio that unfolds chronologically, tying each reflection electronically to a place in the syllabus. The annotations to the syllabus are intended to articulate some of my thinking behind the choices for each week's readings or a particular assignment.

Examining Evidence of Student Learning

Finally, I address both the strengths and the weaknesses of the course, specifically in the context of student work, in a major section called "Learning: A Narrative Analysis." This section gets at a central feature of the course portfolio as a genre: the way it represents evidence about student learning, at least taking a stab at the question of teaching effectiveness in light of impact on student learning.

In this section of the portfolio, my approach to this key issue is to review a number of examples of online student projects in light of certain learning outcomes and behaviors, many of which are desirable and compatible with my goals, but some of which represent lingering concerns. I look at examples of student work that evidence a facility and playfulness with form, a focus on close reading and language, an engagement with dialogic connections either to their peers' work or external sources, and I look for evidence of paradigm shifts that involve thinking about the Web-like interrelatedness of key ideas and themes in the course.

I elaborate on the evidence from students' direct reflections and their work that the course was at least modestly successful in achieving all five of its goals. Most students seemed to feel that they learned something significant about the openness and complexity of form and literary narrative; most students saw continuities between technical and literary aspects of the course and were able to articulate, in their reflections or their projects, significant connections between their engagement with nontraditional and nonlinear narrative paradigms, on the one hand, and narrative and literary complexity, on the other; and finally, for most students, the chance to use electronic tools (and hypertext writing), while difficult for many, was interesting and expansive.

What the Portfolio Can and Cannot Prove

While I am committed to bringing forward evidence about student learning in the portfolio, I would also note that the issue of "proof" is in my mind permanently problematic. Thus, my portfolio also addresses this question outright in a section (it is part of "Argument") entitled "The Burden of Proof":

> What is it that this Course Portfolio is trying to prove, if it is to prove anything at all? One of the productive challenges of writing a Portfolio is the pressure of looking at the evidence of student learning, in light of one's pedagogical intentions, and drawing conclusions about the effectiveness of techniques and approaches. Indeed, that is what I will do in both the Argument and Learning sections. However, in analyzing the data and writing the Portfolio, I found myself asking a larger question regarding the burden of proof on any single course to demonstrate learning outcomes,

> let alone a course working with new tools and approaches that are not to be found elsewhere in a curriculum. Most of what we expect from any given course is contextualized by the recurrence of those same skills or approaches in other courses. Ideally, any major curriculum is characterized by certain common methods and conceptual tools across a course of study. Any introductory course faces a crunch of coverage that has to do with the absence of certain skills to build on.
>
> Similarly, one of the difficulties in teaching this particular course is its multiple agendae: an introduction to American Literary Traditions, critical reading skills, introduction to contexts and approaches to these novels, introduction to nonlinear electronic narrative, a foundational grounding in the Web and other electronic tools, and a functional introduction to writing in hypertext and the construction of Web-based analytic and writing projects. Having taught this course twice, I realize that while there are some things that I can do in terms of time management (e.g., increasing the course from three to four credits), some technical obstacles that can be removed, and some pedagogical adjustments that I can make, one truism will remain: An anomalous course in the curriculum will always be limited in its impact. By this, I simply mean that what can be accomplished in one course is completely different from what could be accomplished if students were encountering some of these skills across several

courses. Given this, my goals for the course are not to do everything with the same level of coverage or rigor but to privilege certain learning goals over others as the primary focus of the course. In the absence of the ability to do everything perfectly, I decided that my main goal for this course would be paradigmatic: Above all else I want students to open up their notions about how literary narrative works by engaging in a whole range of new reading and writing experiences.

Possible Conclusions

I raise this issue about the burden of proof in anticipation of two questions that I hear in many different forms at faculty-development workshops that I have conducted around the country. One question is: What is the evidence that students learn American literature better using computers than with traditional methods? The second question is: Why would you spend time teaching students nonlinear writing and nontraditional textuality when they cannot even write well in traditional, linear ways?

I hope that I respond to both of these questions throughout the portfolio, but I would also make two summary points here. First, one has to look at the use of technology in its whole, ecological context. Whatever impact the technology has in this course is intimately related to other pedagogical and methodological dimensions, many of which have evolved in my teaching through the use of technology. Second, one of the things that I sought to test in designing this course was the notion that one could draw students' attention to the rigors of argument and analysis by engaging them with nonlinear writing and nontraditional texts. As the

portfolio illustrates, my primary premise was to introduce students to a sophisticated set of ideas about narrative and analysis through the use of nonlinear writing and reading tools and concepts. That is, it would be easier to engage their reflection on print narrative and linear argument if they could step outside into some alternatives for perspective. And this is one reason that the balance of traditional and nontraditional, print and electronic, pedagogies is so important to the success of this type of course.

Helping the Reader

Finally, a word about aspects of the portfolio designed to make it easier to read. The hypertext course portfolio contains several navigational tools, including a comprehensive index to course materials, related evaluation data, and the various sections of the course portfolio. Additionally, at the bottom of every page in the course portfolio is a "navigation bar" with each of the portfolio's components accessible through links.

The "Portfolio Navigation Guide and Index" provides links to all of the online documents and pieces comprising the portfolio and the course. These materials range from the "Course Prospectus" to full reflective data from Hypertext Project; to materials I've authored for students to help them visualize nontraditional work, such as the Hypertext Template and Sample *Moby-Dick* Hypertext. Finally, I've written the "Executive Summary," which links to all of the components of the course portfolio and gives an overview of the course itself. Some readers may find it easiest to read the online version with a print copy of this summary in hand.

I welcome any and all feedback on this portfolio, which can be seen at http://www. georgetown.edu/ bassr/portfolio/amlit/.

Audiences and Occasions: Using Course Portfolios for Peer Collaboration and Review of Teaching

Pat Hutchings, Senior Scholar, The Carnegie Foundation for the Advancement of Teaching

A theme evident in reports from faculty who develop course portfolios is that having to explain one's teaching to a reader enforces a kind of self-discipline and attentiveness that is surprisingly powerful. Steve Dunbar, a mathematician from the University of Nebraska-Lincoln, who reported on his course portfolio in an earlier AAHE publication, explains that "knowing that others will review my documentation through the portfolio is a way of keeping myself honest and focused" (1996, 57). Similarly, in case study 5 in this volume, Deborah Langsam talks about the power of the writing process, and the sense of audience implied therein: "Committing my thoughts to paper helps to clarify them and prevents me from skipping past the 'hard parts' (i.e., the places where my thinking is muddy). To explain to others is to explain to myself" (60). But what do we know about those "others" and the sense they make (or don't) of our course portfolios?

This is, understandably, a crucial question in the minds of many faculty and campuses considering course portfolios, because it gets to the issue of costs and benefits: Is it worth the time? Will anybody want to read my portfolio? Will readers be able to make sense of it? learn from it and use it? make judgments about it? Often these questions are framed in the context of tenure, promotion, and merit, which was in fact an essential context for several members of the AAHE Course Portfolio Working Group (see case studies 2, 6, and 9 by Donna Martsolf, Charles Mignon, and Randy Bass). But personnel committees are only one kind of audience in one kind of context. This chapter attempts to open up the question of audiences and occasions more broadly, looking at ways that course portfolios can foster what is now too rare: peer collaboration and review of teaching.

How Readers Read Portfolios

In January of 1996, members of the Working Group agreed to find readers for the portfolios we had developed over the previous year — or rather, to find out whether we could find readers (as in, what if we had portfolios and no one would read them?). We generated the adjacent list of questions about possible purposes and uses of course portfolios and asked our readers to respond to them. Additionally, we learned about the effects of portfolios from other colleagues who have used them, and from an experiment undertaken by one of our long-distance collaborators,

Questions

1. For what purposes and for which audiences might the portfolio be useful?
2. How well does the design and structure of the portfolio work? Do the pieces "hang together"? What's missing?
3. Is it possible to make a judgment about the quality of the teaching and learning documented in the portfolio? What criteria might be applied?
4. What could be done to make the portfolio more readable?

97

Kathleen Quinlan, at the Australian National University. (Her report appears at the end of this chapter.) What did we learn?

First, we learned that *readers were engaged.* The Working Group solicited readers from a range of contexts and roles: a departmental colleague, a colleague across campus in another department, a scholar in the field from another campus, a department chair, a provost. . . . Virtually all of these readers reported that they found the portfolio interesting and engaging. Even allowing for what may have been good manners in part, their comments are heartening. A colleague in another English department who provided an external review of Charles Mignon's American literature course portfolio wrote, "I found Charles's portfolio stimulating to read and highly worthy of emulation." Deborah Langsam reports that "reviewers understood the developmental nature of the portfolio and seemed to value the potential benefits of the process to the individual instructor and to the overall improvement of instruction" (this volume, 61).

Interestingly, in light of our concern about length, several readers wanted more. One reader (a colleague from the same field as that represented in the portfolio) noted, "Here I am, with an armload more of insight [into this person's teaching] than I ever had before, and yet I want *more.*" The same reader noted that the portfolio gave her a sense of being involved in the course in an immediate, personal way: "I felt somehow in the midst of the course, moving *through* it with you." A historian who read William Cutler's portfolio about a survey of American history course noted, "If the point is to get someone interested in taking your course, then you succeeded. It sounds intellectually very challenging and exciting."

Second, we found that *readers saw real and immediate usefulness* in the portfolios — beyond the usefulness to the portfolio developer, that is. One reviewer wrote, "[T]he reader of this [portfolio] is likely to come away from the reading with some ideas for better teaching." A reader of Deborah Langsam's plant biology course portfolio noted, "[S]ince I teach the complementary introductory course in animal biology, I was most interested in the approaches you use to stimulate student interest."

Many readers also imagined benefits beyond those they themselves might reap. William Cutler notes that a colleague who read his portfolio in a personnel decision-making context not only was able to use it to make judgments (see the following discussion) but also found that "my portfolio might serve an institutional purpose by acting as a model for graduate students and junior colleagues preparing to teach this course for the first time" (this volume, 21). (This purpose informs a course portfolio initiative begun by engineering graduate students at the University of Wisconsin, reported in the box opposite.) Similarly, a reader of Deborah Langsam's portfolio writes that

University of Wisconsin-Madison College of Engineering

Like many programs, the College of Engineering at the University of Wisconsin-Madison sees considerable turnover among TAs, making it difficult for the program to learn from and build on teaching practice from semester to semester. To address this problem, a group of TAs recently proposed and pioneered the writing of course portfolios.

The contents of these portfolios are familiar: an account of course goals, learning activities, assessments, and examples of student work. What makes them different is that they "belong" not to the individual TA but to the program, becoming part of a public resource for subsequent TAs there.

Benefits of the course portfolios are currently under study, but early experience suggests that the process of their development helps TAs reflect on their teaching and their students' learning. Additionally, portfolios are expected to be useful in accreditation.

For a look at the program's handbook for creating a course portfolio, see http://www.cae.wisc.edu/~tafellow. Click on "Previous TA Fellows and Their Projects," then on "Course Portfolio Development," and finally on "Handbook for Creating Course Portfolios." You will need Acrobat Reader to view the handbook file.

"although it contains many personal reflections, [the portfolio] also provides valuable information which could be shared, as a guideline, with other professors teaching the course, as well as given to new professors teaching the course for the first time." This reader went on, in fact, to imagine that each department might have "a library of teaching portfolios available for each of the courses taught in the department." A different audience was envisioned by a reader who reported that he and his colleagues were trying to develop syllabi for "external audiences that would give them a good picture of how we actually approach teaching our courses." He saw the course portfolio as a strategy for this kind of communication with constituencies beyond the campus — potential students, accreditors, policymakers, and individuals studying higher education.

Third (though part and parcel of the second point above), *readers saw the portfolio as an occasion for creating a culture of teaching and learning.* In chapter 1 of this volume, Lee Shulman talks about the power of texts to create communities of discourse, and this is an effect that has emerged in a number of settings. The Working Group itself is one example. All of us found the group an occasion for serious substantive exchange about teaching and learning that was unusual, even unprecedented, in our careers. And we were struck by examples from beyond our group that reinforced this point. For instance, the history department at the University of Georgia used William Cutler's portfolio as a prompt for a teaching circle.

We also uncovered interesting variations on the course portfolio that seem particularly powerful for community-building. Seven chemistry faculty members at the University of Michigan (some 30 percent of the department) set up a regular seminar organized around "oral portfolios." These exchanges were particularly useful in fostering shared understandings of course goals and teaching approaches (see the box opposite). Faculty in the University of Nebraska-Lincoln math department developed what one member called "a collective course portfolio" documenting their teaching (each in his or her own section) of a newly revised calculus course. (The portfolio is available on its website at http://www.math.unl.edu. Click on "Course Materials," then on "Math 106/107/208," and lastly on "Instructor Notes." The portfolio file is in TeX format and requires TeX software for viewing.)

Finally, we found that *readers were able to make some judgments about quality.* This was important even though not all members of the Working Group intended their portfolios for personnel decisions; all of us, nevertheless, hoped that readers would be able to make critical judgments on the basis of our investigations and documentation — a prerequisite, after all, for any kind of thoughtful feedback and response.

The Oral Portfolio Approach

Benefits

- Encouraged faculty to devote time to reflection on goals, approaches, etc.
- Required a time commitment (both to develop and to review the portfolios) below any "rejection threshold"
- Demonstrated that talking about teaching is a legitimate activity
- Dramatically improved communication within the department about course objectives
- Provided useful formative feedback

Limits

- Less time was spent in reflection than might have been spent with a written portfolio
- Presentations were probably less open regarding teaching problems than a private memo might be
- Limited student input (offset by mid-semester evaluations, which the group also employed as a complement to the portfolios)
- Not useful as a summative tool

James Penner-Hahn, Chemistry, University of Michigan

For some readers the task of judgment was apparently unproblematic: William Cutler reports, "the two members of my department who reviewed [the portfolio] said that it provided them with a welcome means by which to judge my teaching" (this volume, 21). Orin Chein's provost (who is also a mathematician) read Chein's portfolio and responded that it should "go a long way towards helping me make a good evaluation of the quality of [Chein's] teaching and the amount of student learning in this course" (this volume, 45). In his external peer review of Charles Mignon's portfolio, Larry Andrews wrote,

> *I feel that I have a much wider basis for judging Charles's teaching than I would have had solely from student evaluations and two or three class visit reports by colleagues — the traditional evidence of teaching. What is suddenly visible here is his teaching mind — always planning, assessing, daring, questioning, growing.*

One reader noted that although she would not use Deborah Langsam's professional-development portfolio as an evaluative instrument in a promotion and tenure context, she "would use the portfolio to inform the rest of the teaching data provided, e.g., student evaluations, peer observations, chair observation."

Such comments notwithstanding, readers were much more skeptical about the usefulness of course portfolios for high-stakes decisions than for other purposes mentioned above. A reader of my portfolio noted, for instance, that she could not, on the basis of the portfolio alone (though it contains many samples of student work), "speak confidently" about what seemed to her to matter most: "what happened for your students in this course." Judging quality turns out to be quite problematic.

But it is important to note that the problem here may not lie primarily in portfolio design and substance. After all, the possibility of judgment depends on a conception of excellence against which the teaching and learning depicted in the portfolio can be judged. As Mary Huber notes in chapter 3, relevant frameworks for evaluation *have* been put forward, including the one in *Scholarship Assessed.* (One of Charles Mignon's readers used its framework.) There is also a considerable literature on the subject of effective teaching that could be distilled and used to guide reading and reviews. However, the question, What constitutes excellent teaching? is not one that will be settled by a list or framework; it is a situated, contextual question to which the answer is almost inevitably, It depends — on the particulars of the subject, programmatic context, students, physical setting, etc. Indeed, one of the arguments for course portfolios is that they capture the particulars of the context, rather than treating teaching as a generic act.

To put it differently, the question behind a portfolio is not, Is this person a good teacher? but, How did *this* iteration of the design and teaching of *this* course work for *these* students? And the answer to this second question is not likely to be a simple yes or no — or a score of 4.3. What portfolios do is, in fact, usefully to complicate the process of judgment by putting further, richer evidence into the picture, especially evidence about the substance of teaching, which, as Keig and Waggoner (1994) point out, is shortchanged when student ratings are the only game in town: "When faculty and administrators allow student ratings to be the only real source of information about teaching, they unwittingly contribute to a system in which too much emphasis is placed on evaluating superficial teaching skills and not enough is placed on more substantive matters" (1). The aim of teaching portfolios and course portfolios is not, it should be said, to replace student voices. Nor can they be seen as a panacea to the evaluation problem (which remains, as it always will, a process of expert judgment, not a matter of applying a measuring stick). But at their best, portfolios supplement, complement, round out the picture, especially as related to the substance of teaching and its effects on student learning.

Six Suggestions for Making Portfolios Useful to Readers

Kathleen Quinlan, whose report begins on the next page, has said that while "course portfolios are, like a personal diary, helpful to the faculty member who prepares one, they are generally, unlike a diary, meant to be read and commented on by others." If portfolios are to deliver on their promises in this regard — as tools for peer collaboration and review of teaching — the following suggestions may be helpful.

1. Include in the portfolio itself a clear statement of intended purpose.

2. Provide readers with all possible aids and guides. As noted in chapter 4, these might include a table of contents, overview or executive summary, tabs, color-coding, etc.

3. Involve readers (or potential readers) in decisions about portfolio design and use. Decisions about what to include, how much, and for what purpose need to be discussed and negotiated — and revised on the basis of ongoing experimentation and practice. This is particularly crucial where portfolios are likely to be used in high-stakes decision making.

4. Make rubrics and frameworks for review explicit. No checklist can capture the richness of a portfolio; one of the reasons to use portfolios is the messy, qualitative, idiosyncratic picture they paint of teaching and learning. But it may nevertheless be helpful to have some guiding questions or categories for reading — that is, some standards or criteria for what a reader might expect to see addressed in the portfolio. Alternatively, the reader might be asked to set forward and make explicit the criteria he or she uses (see, for instance, the criteria proposed by Charles Mignon's reviewer, Larry Andrews, in the box opposite).

5. Create occasions to build expert judgment. A frequent objection to portfolios is that faculty do not have the training necessary to assess one another's practice. True enough. But useful models for training and building frameworks for review can be found, for instance in composition studies, where the process of "norming" the evaluation of student writing is well established.

6. Report and learn from our experiences. Progress with portfolio use requires scholarly study and documentation of the experiences of real readers, which is why this chapter concludes with a report on one such experiment.

> ## One Reader's Criteria for Evaluation
>
> 1. clarity and logic of portfolio organization
> 2. scholarly tone, critically distanced
> 3. intelligence and thoughtful analysis in the planning, executing, and assessment of teaching
> 4. evidence of student-centered learning
> 5. evidence of up-to-date expertise in the field
> 6. evidence of ongoing intellectual and personal growth as a teacher
>
> *Larry Andrews, English, Kent State University*

A Study of the Reading of Course Portfolios

by Kathleen Quinlan[4]

As members of the AAHE Course Portfolio Working Group were developing their portfolios, sending them off to readers, and reflecting on their reviewer's response, I designed a study from a different angle to look systematically at how academics who were unfamiliar with course portfolios read and interpreted a colleague's course portfolio. Two main questions guided this study:

1. Which parts of the portfolio did the reviewers pay most attention to?

2. How or by what processes did readers review their colleague's portfolio?

The first question is important to those teachers developing portfolios because length is always an issue. We want them to be rich and thorough, and we want them to contain artifacts and reflections about several components of teaching, yet they must not overwhelm the reader. Which parts, then, did a group of readers pay the most attention to and consider most important?

The second question is prompted by the concern that most faculty are not well versed in pedagogy or educational evaluation. This concern has been frequently voiced by opponents to the peer review of teaching. A related concern is that the peer's evaluations will be based unduly on personal biases for or against particular styles of teaching. I wanted to learn how and whether these concerns affected the reading and judging of portfolios.

How the Study Was Conducted

Fyfe Bygrave, a biochemistry professor at the Australian National University, and I developed a concise portfolio focused on his course Biochemistry of Metabolism and Its Regulation, a second-year science course in the department of Biochemistry and Molecular Biology. The portfolio contained Fyfe's self-reflection on the course; the syllabus; a sample of a summary of lecture notes handed out to students; a sample tutorial test; sample instructions for write-up on the tutorial practical; guidelines for an essay assignment; the final examination; and results of student evaluations of teaching.

Because the study design involved subjects reading the portfolio in a face-to-face, think-aloud interview, the portfolio had to be short to ensure an interview of reasonable length. Therefore, the portfolio items were in part selected for brevity. Examples of student work were not included. The

[4] I acknowledge the support of a New Starters Grant from The Faculties, the Australian National University, which helped fund this study. I also thank the academics who volunteered to participate in the study, particularly Professor Fyfe Bygrave.

total length of the portfolio was 31 pages of large-print material, more than a third of which contained diagrams and tables rather than substantial amounts of text. These circumstances meant that the portfolio was shorter than many of the ones described in the case studies in this volume.

With the portfolio complete, we invited seven faculty members from the department of Biochemistry and Molecular Biology to participate in individual interviews in which they each read and thought out loud about the portfolio. The interviewees all knew Fyfe and were familiar to some degree with how the course fit into the department's curriculum. In the interviews, which typically lasted 90 minutes, each interviewee was briefed on the purpose of the study and asked to read the portfolio with this hypothetical task in mind:

> *The university is initiating a new award for teaching based on excellence in a particular course. To be granted an award, applicants must select one of their courses through which to demonstrate excellence in teaching . . . and you have been asked to be one of the reviewers for this new award program. . . . The university has given reviewers considerable freedom to define "excellence in teaching" in ways that are appropriate to each discipline. Therefore, it is important that you explain your evaluation and how you reach your decision.*
>
> *How would you evaluate the following unit? Would you recommend it for the award? Why or why not? On what grounds do you make your case?*

The faculty interviewees were instructed to think out loud about their response to the material as they were reading. Each interview was taped and transcribed verbatim. After reading the portfolio and making a judgment about whether he or she would give the teaching of the unit an award for excellence, each interviewee completed two questionnaires, which asked for reflection on the process of reading the portfolio and on what contents he or she would like to see in a course portfolio generally.

What Did the Readers Pay Most Attention To?

To answer this first question, I looked at two sources of information. First, I analyzed the questionnaire results in which participants rated the importance of each of the items in the portfolio. In this, student evaluations were rated most important for determining whether to grant an award; the teacher's self-reflection ranked second; the syllabus and the guidelines for students on writing the essay assignment also rated highly.

For the second source, I treated the percentage of words spoken by the readers about each section of the portfolio as an indicator of attentiveness to that section. I divided each transcript into sections that matched the sections of the portfolio, ran a word count for each of the sections, and calculated what percentage of words in the entire interview was devoted to each of the items in the portfolio. Overall, readers thought out loud most about the self-reflection by the teacher and the syllabus.

On both of these measures, then, self-reflection and course design (the syllabus) were highly valued. This would seem to accord with the experiences reported by faculty in the case studies in this volume (though they also placed a high premium on student work, not included in Fyfe's portfolio).

What Processes Did the Faculty Use in Judging the Portfolios?

The instructions gave little guidance and no criteria for the reading and review of the portfolios; readers were asked to provide their own justifications for the judgments they arrived at. Not surprisingly, readers thus relied on idiosyncratic, implicit criteria. Some placed greater emphasis on the teacher's apparent concern for students. Those with greater familiarity with the content area spent more time discussing the degree of curricular coherence or the balance of topics presented. A reader with a specialty in science education discussed how science was represented and the epistemological assumptions underpinning the pedagogical choices made.

The most common strategy that the faculty readers used, however, was to test Fyfe's teaching against their own practice and experiences. The readers seemed to be asking themselves, Would I do it this way? They used phrases such as "I agree with this" and "That's exactly the sort of approach that I think I would take." Also common were explicit statements of "I would/wouldn't do that," as well as shifts to describing what they themselves do in their own classes. These kinds of comments were given in response to every aspect of the teacher's materials in the portfolio, including the level of detail in the lecture notes, the use of an essay, the construction of the final exam, and the logic of the course content and design. Generally, if the practice accorded with what the reviewer does or "would do," it was evaluated positively. If the reviewers wouldn't themselves do it that way, then typically Fyfe's practice or approach was evaluated negatively or with some indecision as they weighed pros and cons.

The readers, then, did bring their own values, experiences, biases, and interests into the reviewing process. It may be difficult for reviewers to acknowledge a practice as very different from their own preferred style or approach to teaching and still see that practice as effectively contributing to student learning.

Additional Factors That Influenced Readers' Judgments

In addition to comparing against their own practice, Fyfe's readers often compared what was presented in the portfolio with their image of "traditional" or "usual" practice in science teaching. For some, the assumption seemed to be that an award for excellence would require innovation. Thus, the relationship between excellence, innovation, and traditional practice was unclear.

Some readers also made judgments related to their sense of course context. Several of them seemed to hold visions of "the ideal" in their heads that represented an absolute standard of excellence. Some were willing to adjust this ideal standard by taking into account situational constraints such as time, space, and equipment; others wanted to hold fast to their high standards. An implication here is that teachers developing portfolios might want to address the circumstances in which they teach and what situational constraints they perceive as affecting their pedagogical choices; that is, they might head the reader off at the pass by articulating their own ideal and describing any constraints that they believe might have necessitated compromises to that ideal.

Not surprisingly, readers' inside knowledge was also sometimes brought to bear. As noted above, all seven readers were members of Fyfe's department. (This approach made sense since the first level of peer review in many summative contexts requires nomination and approval of the department, or at least the department head or chair.) I was interested in learning how readers integrate information about the teacher and the course that they have acquired from other interactions beyond the reading of the portfolio. One way was to apply their understandings about how the course was organized, and the departmental decisions behind its present design.

Second, readers brought to bear informal student feedback gathered through chats with students rather than through the formal student evaluation of teaching presented in the portfolio. A third source of evidence that the departmental colleagues could use was direct observation; several of the reviewers had had the opportunity to observe Fyfe's teaching, and they mentioned their impressions from such observations. These interactions clearly allowed interpretations that went beyond the information available in the brief portfolio.

It is apparent, then, that the reviewers were not relying solely on the information presented in the portfolio. In some cases, their knowledge of the department added layers of interpretation and meaning to the sketchy information in the portfolio. In other cases, before looking at the portfolio the reviewers seemed to have already formed a judgment about a particular practice they had observed or heard about from students. Sometimes, though, the portfolio gave them a context for the teacher's intentions, which allowed them a richer understanding of the practice than they might have had before and even changed their prior, less-informed assessments.

Practical Implications

This evidence points to the importance of the teacher's self-reflection and contextualizing comments. For readers who already have some awareness of the portfolio author's practices and students' anecdotal reactions to it, understanding the teacher's thinking behind the practices is an important perspective to add. For reviewers outside the department who do not have such awareness, the portfolio will need to contain additional contextual information.

Evidence about this reliance on other sources of information suggests, too, that a course portfolio may not be sufficient information to make a summative judgment about teaching. For those arguing for more information about teaching, it is worth remembering that the portfolio adds perspectives and information, which might hitherto have been unavailable. While imperfect, the portfolio still provides a much fuller picture of a faculty member's teaching than mere anecdotal evidence, summaries of student ratings forms, or one or two unsystematic classroom observations.

A final observation made of the study participants was that they didn't simply accept at face value what was presented in the portfolio. For example, most of the reviewers questioned one or more of the claims made by the teacher —that he memorized all the names of the students, that he could get "candid views of students" from informal face-to-face feedback. . . . Portfolio skeptics often raise concerns that "glossy materials" or slick talk will become more important than the content of the portfolios or the quality of the teaching represented. Yet, this study showed that readers were disposed to question and insist on evidence. Thus, a tidy, well-written portfolio may be necessary, but aesthetics and writing style will not be sufficient if the content is not credible and well supported.

Works Cited

Angelo, Thomas A., and K. Patricia Cross. 1993. *Classroom Assessment Techniques: A Handbook for College Teachers.* 2d ed. San Francisco: Jossey-Bass.

Batson, Trent, and Randy Bass. March/April 1996. "Teaching and Learning in the Computer Age: Primacy of Process." *Change* 28 (2): 42-47.

Berube, Michael. 1996. "Public Perceptions of Universities and Faculty." *Academe* 82: 10-17.

Boyer, Ernest L. 1990. *Scholarship Reconsidered: Priorities of the Professoriate.* Princeton, NJ: Carnegie Foundation for the Advancement of Teaching.

Braskamp, Larry A., and John C. Ory. 1994. *Assessing Faculty Work: Enhancing Individual and Institutional Performance.* San Francisco: Jossey-Bass.

Carnegie Foundation for the Advancement of Teaching. 1997. "Proposal for the Carnegie Teaching Academy to The Pew Charitable Trusts." Duplicated.

Cerbin, William. 1996. "Inventing a New Genre: The Course Portfolio at the University of Wisconsin-La Crosse." In *Making Teaching Community Property: A Menu for Peer Collaboration and Peer Review,* edited by Pat Hutchings, pp. 52-56. Washington, DC: American Association for Higher Education.

Clements, Kendrick A. April 1988. "Promotion and Tenure for Public Historians." *Organization of American Historians Council of Chairs Newsletter,* 6.

Diamond, Robert M., and Bronwyn E. Adam, eds. 1995. *The Disciplines Speak: Rewarding the Scholarly, Professional, and Creative Work of Faculty.* Washington, DC: American Association for Higher Education.

Dunbar, Steve. 1996. "Developing a Course Portfolio in Math: A Report From the University of Nebraska-Lincoln. In *Making Teaching Community Property: A Menu for Peer Collaboration and Peer Review,* edited by Pat Hutchings, pp. 56-58. Washington, DC: American Association for Higher Education.

Edgerton, Russell. 1996. "Preface." In *Making Teaching Community Property: A Menu for Peer Collaboration and Peer Review,* edited by Pat Hutchings, pp. v-vii. Washington, DC: American Association for Higher Education.

Glassick, Charles E., Mary Taylor Huber, and Gene I. Maeroff. 1997. *Scholarship Assessed: Evaluation of the Professoriate.* A special report of the Carnegie Foundation for the Advancement of Teaching. San Francisco: Jossey-Bass.

Huber, Mary Taylor. 1997. "What Makes Public Scholarship 'Public'?" Paper presented to the Seminar on Public Scholarship, Graduate Institute of the Liberal Arts, 26 March, Emory University, Atlanta.

Hutchings, Pat, ed. 1996. *Making Teaching Community Property: A Menu for Peer Collaboration and Peer Review.* Washington, DC: American Association for Higher Education.

Keig, Larry, and Michael D. Waggoner. 1994. *Collaborative Peer Review: The Role of Faculty in Improving College Teaching.* ASHE-ERIC Higher Education Reports, no. 2. Washington, DC: The George Washington University, School of Education and Human Development.

Lauter, Paul, ed. 1990. *Heath Anthology of American Literature. Vol. 2.* Lexington, MA: D.C. Heath.

Lynton, Ernest A. 1995. *Making the Case for Professional Service.* Washington, DC: American Association for Higher Education.

McMillan, J.H. 1988. *Assessing Students' Learning.* New Directions for Teaching and Learning, no. 34. San Francisco: Jossey-Bass.

Millis, Barbara. 1995. "Shaping the Reflective Portfolio: A Philosophical Look at the Mentoring Role." *Journal on Excellence in College Teaching* 6 (1): 65-73.

Perkins, D. 1992. *Smart Schools: From Training Memories to Educating Minds.* New York: Free Press.

Rice, R. Eugene. 1995. "Welcome to the Conference!" Program to the AAHE Conference on Faculty Roles & Rewards, "From 'My Work' to 'Our Work': Realigning Faculty Work With College and University Purposes," 19-22 January, Phoenix, AZ.

Shulman, Lee S. November/December 1993. "Teaching as Community Property: Putting an End to Pedagogical Solitude." *Change* 25 (6): 6-7.

———, Steven R. Dunbar, and Gary Sandefur. 1996. "Capturing the Scholarship in Teaching: The Course Portfolio." Presentation at the AAHE Conference on Faculty Roles & Rewards, 21 January, Atlanta. [An audiotape of this session (#96CFRR-63) is available from the Mobiltape Company; call 1-800/369-5718.]

Tompkins, Jane. October 1990. "Pedagogy of the Distressed." *College English* 52: 653-60.

Walvoord, B.E., and V.J. Anderson. 1998. *Effective Grading: A Tool for Learning and Assessment.* San Francisco: Jossey-Bass.

Wiggins, G. 1998. *Educative Assessment: Designing Assessments to Inform and Improve Student Performance.* San Francisco: Jossey-Bass.

Wilson, Woodrow. 1961. "Princeton in the Nation's Service." In *American Higher Education: A Documentary History. Vol. 2.*, edited by Richard Hofstadter and Wilson Smith, pp. 684-95. Chicago: University of Chicago Press.

Wiske, M.S., ed. 1998. *Teaching for Understanding.* San Francisco: Jossey-Bass.

Resources for Further Work

*Laurie Milford, Project Assistant, and Pat Hutchings, Senior Scholar,
The Carnegie Foundation for the Advancement of Teaching*

The use of portfolios has, over the last several years, generated a considerable body of literature and resources. What follows here is by no means an exhaustive listing of what is available; our intention, rather, is to point readers toward a first level of information, which will in turn point to additional sources. Some of the items appear in Works Cited, but many do not.

Resources that deal centrally with course portfolios or teaching portfolios appear in the first section; the second section includes other items of interest, particularly those related to the conceptual foundation for work on the course portfolio (new conceptions of scholarship, for instance) or strategies and processes related to the portfolio's development and use (classroom assessment, for example, and ways to foster thoughtful public discourse about teaching and learning).

For simplicity's sake, online materials are listed separately, in a final section. With the exception of the volume's case study authors, we have not listed websites of individual faculty, no matter how portfolio-like or how interesting those sites might have been. Instead, we have attempted to list sites that represent larger collective efforts and products related to the scholarship of teaching and learning.

Resources About Course Portfolios and/or Teaching Portfolios

Anderson, Erin, ed. 1993. *Campus Use of the Teaching Portfolio: Twenty-Five Profiles.* Washington, DC: American Association for Higher Education.

> Two- to three-page accounts of how 25 campuses have used teaching portfolios: why, on what model, with what impact, etc. Includes sample campus materials (e.g., guidelines to faculty specifying what might go into the portfolio, scoring rubrics, and names of contact persons). The publication predates the interest in course portfolios, but many of the purposes and principles behind campus use of the teaching portfolio also pertain to its cousin, the course portfolio.

Cambridge, Barbara L. 1996. "The Paradigm Shifts: Examining Quality of Teaching Through Assessment of Student Learning." *Innovative Higher Education* 20 (4): 287-98.

> Like proponents of the course portfolio, Cambridge argues that learning is the chief goal of teaching and that faculty can thus assess teaching through analysis of student work. She is particularly interested in the power of involving students in this process, and describes, therefore, three practices that bring together faculty, faculty peers, and students as partners in assessing teaching and learning. Both student and teacher portfolios play a role in what Cambridge proposes.

Centra, John A. 1993. *Reflective Faculty Evaluation*. San Francisco: Jossey-Bass.
Promoting active teaching and arguing that it needs to be evaluated with
nontraditional methods, Centra offers new ways to engage both teachers
and students in the improvement of the teaching practice. He describes the
importance of portfolios in this endeavor.

Cerbin, William. 1994. "The Course Portfolio as a Tool for Continuous
Improvement of Teaching and Learning." *Journal on Excellence in College
Teaching* 5: 95-105.
Argues for assessment of teaching that takes into account information
about student learning. Proposes the course portfolio as a vehicle for revealing and analyzing the teaching-learning relationship. As several chapters
here in this volume noted, Cerbin is a pioneer of the course portfolio.

——— . 1995. "Connecting Assessment of Learning to Improvement of
Teaching Through the Course Portfolio." *Assessment Update* 7 (1): 4-6.
Argues for what Cerbin calls "learner-centered evaluation," a concept that
he then illustrates through an excerpt from his own course portfolio,
focused on a classroom activity employing student groups. Other articles in
this issue of *Assessment Update* might also be of interest, in that all of them
focus on ways to promote a more reflective community of practice for
teachers.

Cutler, William W., III. 1997. "The History Course Portfolio." *Perspectives* 35 (8):
17-20.
Cutler describes how historians can use course portfolios to organize and
display the argument behind decisions about the format and substance of
individual courses. He describes different approaches to portfolios and the
benefits of building them — both to the individual teacher of history and to
the field. *Perspectives* is the newsletter of the American Historical
Association. (Cutler's own portfolio is available online through the AHA
website; see below.)

Edgerton, Russell, Patricia Hutchings, and Kathleen Quinlan. 1991. *The
Teaching Portfolio: Capturing the Scholarship in Teaching*. Washington, DC:
American Association for Higher Education.
Argues for teaching portfolios based on a conception of teaching as scholarly work for which faculty have a professional responsibility to ensure and
improve quality. Calls for portfolios organized around the "key tasks of
teaching," and provides eight sample entries that document effectiveness
on such tasks.

Georgi, D., and J. Crow. 1998. "Digital Portfolios: A Confluence of Portfolio
Assessment and Technology." *Teacher Education Quarterly* 25 (1): 73-84.
Primary focus is actually on student portfolios, but the article (and several

others in this specially edited issue of *TEQ)* is useful in its attention to hypertext as a medium for portfolios — an approach advocated here in this volume by Randy Bass.

Hutchings, Pat, ed. 1996. *Making Teaching Community Property: A Menu for Peer Collaboration and Peer Review.* Washington, DC: American Association for Higher Education.

This 1996 volume describes nine strategies through which faculty can make their work as teachers available to one another — be it for individual improvement, for building the collective wisdom of practice in the field, or for personnel decision making. Strategies include, among others, teaching circles, reciprocal classroom observations, team teaching, and external peer review. Chapter 5 is dedicated to course portfolios; it includes reports from two faculty who have used the method: William Cerbin, whose pioneering work was essential to members of the AAHE Course Portfolio Working Group, and Steve Dunbar, a member of that AAHE group.

———, ed. 1995. *From Idea to Prototype: The Peer Review of Teaching (A Project Workbook).* Washington, DC: American Association for Higher Education.

A collection of materials, examples, and tasks developed through a national project on the peer review of teaching. Material behind tab four focuses on the course portfolio as a way of "putting the pieces together," and provides two full portfolios: one by Eli Passow, whose case study of that portfolio appears here in this volume; the other by Henry Binford, professor of history at Northwestern University, focused on the first half of a two-quarter course on the development of the modern American city. Also note that the *Project Workbook* contains the "three exercises" referred to by several case study authors here in this volume as the starting point for their portfolios.

Malik, David J. 1994. "Peer Review of Teaching: External Review of Course Content." *Innovative Higher Education* 20 (4): 277-86.

Recounts efforts in the chemistry department at Indiana University Purdue University Indianapolis to institute, on a pilot basis, a new approach to the evaluation of teaching, designed to supplement student ratings and to provide the kind of external scholarly perspective employed with research. Malik does not talk about course portfolios per se, but the evidence assembled and sent for external review ("course description, syllabus, reflective memo") will be familiar to those acquainted with course portfolios. Particularly useful are Malik's comments about new insights and different perspectives gleaned from external reviewers' comments.

Richlin, Laurie, and Milton D. Cox, eds. 1995. *Journal on Excellence in College Teaching* 6 (1).

The issue is dedicated almost exclusively to the teaching portfolio and contains a number of useful essays. Of particular relevance to the course portfolio, however, are essays by Barbara Millis ("Shaping the Reflective

Portfolio") and by Ronald Smith ("Creating a Culture of Teaching Through the Teaching Portfolio").

Seldin, Peter. 1991. *The Teaching Portfolio: A Practical Guide to Improved Performance and Promotion/Tenure Decisions*. Bolton, MA: Anker.
> Along with general guidelines and arguments for portfolios, Seldin offers 17 sample teaching portfolios from disciplines including education, biology, English, history, mathematics, and religion.

————. 1993. *Successful Use of Teaching Portfolios*. Bolton, MA: Anker.
> In this and his previous book on the subject, *The Teaching Portfolio* (1991), Seldin reports on his extensive work with campuses attempting to introduce teaching portfolios for various purposes.

Shulman, Lee S., Steven R. Dunbar, and Gary Sandefur. 1996. "Capturing the Scholarship in Teaching: The Course Portfolio." Presentation at the AAHE Conference on Faculty Roles & Rewards, 21 January, Atlanta.
> Dunbar, a mathematician at the University of Nebraska-Lincoln, and Sandefur, a sociologist from the University of Wisconsin-Madison, discuss early efforts at designing course portfolios; Shulman's opening and closing commentaries provide for the two presenters' work a conceptual framework and rationale (which is echoed in chapter 2 here in this volume). [An audio-tape of the session (#96CFRR-63) can be purchased from the Mobiltape Company; call 1-800/369-5718.]

Other Resources Relevant to the Development and Use of the Course Portfolio

American Assembly of Collegiate Schools of Business. 1997. "Peer Review of Teaching: A Strategy for Improving Teaching and Learning." Produced by AACSB, 20 February. Videocassette.
> Participants in this network-quality videoconference discuss strategies for documenting and reviewing the scholarship of teaching, and the experiences of business schools participating in AAHE's national project From Idea to Prototype: The Peer Review of Teaching. Course portfolios are discussed very briefly. [This video can be purchased at the AACSB website: http://www.aacsb.edu. Click on "Workshops and Seminars," then "Video Conferences," and finally "Order Form for Videotapes."]

Angelo, Thomas A., and K. Patricia Cross. 1993. *Classroom Assessment Techniques: A Handbook for College Teachers*. 2d ed. San Francisco: Jossey-Bass.
> A hefty but well-organized, user-friendly account of strategies that faculty can use to collect feedback from students in order to made midcourse corrections; each strategy comes with examples from a range of disciplines. The volume operates on the premise that faculty can use classroom assessment and classroom research to answer their own questions about their own students' learning (as many of the faculty reporting here in this volume have done).

Barr, Robert B., and John Tagg. November/December 1995. "From Teaching to Learning — A New Paradigm for Undergraduate Education." *Change* 27 (6): 12-25.

Probably the most circulated, cited account of what it means to focus on learning as "a test of teaching." Very much in keeping with the course portfolio's emphasis on evidence about student learning, Barr and Tagg call for a shift from the instruction paradigm to the learning paradigm in which both faculty and students are responsible for the amount and quality of student learning. "The learning paradigm envisions the institution itself as a learner — over time, it continuously learns how to produce more learning with each graduating class, each entering student" (14). Perhaps course portfolios can contribute to this kind of institutional learning, though Barr and Tagg don't take up this question.

Boyer, Ernest L. 1990. *Scholarship Reconsidered: Priorities of the Professoriate.* Princeton, NJ: Carnegie Foundation for the Advancement of Teaching.

Argues for a broader conception of scholarship, encompassing not only basic research (the "scholarship of discovery") but also integration, application, and teaching. Boyer's report has motivated many reexaminations of faculty work in campus-wide projects as well as in the disciplines. Certainly it stands behind the concept of the course portfolio, which treats teaching as scholarly work, entailing systematic investigation, documentation, and review.

Brookfield, Stephen D. 1995. *Becoming a Critically Reflective Teacher.* San Francisco: Jossey-Bass.

"Critically reflective teaching happens," Brookfield tells us, "when we identify and scrutinize the assumptions that undergird how we work" (xii). He suggests four "lenses" for getting at and investigating these underlying (and often problematic) assumptions, including teacher autobiography, the perspective of students, the perspectives of colleagues, and the theoretical literature on pedagogy.

Cross, K. Patricia. December 1990. "Teachers as Scholars." *AAHE Bulletin* 43 (4): 3-5.

A brief and eloquent statement of the idea central to course portfolios: that faculty would do well to think of their classes as "laboratories" for investigating the process of student learning.

——— , and Mimi Harris Steadman. 1996. *Classroom Research: Implementing the Scholarship of Teaching.* San Francisco: Jossey-Bass.

An argument (as in the previous item just above) that faculty can and should investigate their own practice and students' learning. Here, however, readers will find three extended case studies of how such investigations might be undertaken, along with a culminating chapter on "Designing Your Own Classroom Research."

Diamond, Robert M., and Bronwyn E. Adam, eds. 1995. *The Disciplines Speak: Rewarding the Scholarly, Professional, and Creative Work of Faculty.* Washington, DC: American Association for Higher Education.

> Reproduces statements on rewarding faculty work from nine disciplinary/professional societies — religion, history, geography, math, chemistry, the arts, business, journalism, and family/consumer science, plus the National Education Association. A central cross-cutting theme is that teaching is substantive, intellectual work, deserving the time and attention of faculty, careful evaluation, and institutional rewards. (Not surprisingly, in light of such statements, a number of scholarly societies have provided outlets and visibility for faculty in the AAHE Course Portfolio Working Group and AAHE's Peer Review of Teaching project.)

Duffy, Donna Killian, and Janet Wright Jones. 1995. *Teaching Within the Rhythms of the Semester.* San Francisco: Jossey-Bass.

> A rare look at the unfolding of the teaching and learning process over the course of the semester. Especially pertinent, therefore, to the second component of portfolio design: the enactment of the course. Additionally, Duffy and Jones recount their use of portfolios as a dynamic tool for faculty development — a way of charting the progress and impact of classroom assignments and activities.

Edgerton, Russell. September/October 1994. "A National Market for Excellence in Teaching." *Change* 26 (5): 4-5.

> Edgerton argues that "excellent teachers don't have to live out their careers as unknowns, victims of a national market that only recognizes scholars who write publications." He proposes three conditions under which a national market for teaching excellence might be established: a visible product representing teaching excellence, peer judgment, and new forms of public recognition.

Elbow, Peter. Spring 1992. "Making Better Use of Student Evaluations of Teachers." *Association of Departments of English Bulletin* 101: 2-8.

> Elbow answers common objections to asking students what's working (and not) in the classroom. And he provides suggestions for making student evaluations more "trustworthy" and informative. Along the way, he also proposes a number of principles of evaluation that apply equally to student and peer evaluation. For example, he argues, "We can get along with much less official, careful, high-stakes, institutional evaluation of teachers . . . if we make more use of low-stakes evaluation" (4). Many of Elbow's points might guide thoughtful use of course portfolios.

Glassick, Charles E., Mary Taylor Huber, and Gene I. Maeroff. 1997. *Scholarship Assessed: Evaluation of the Professoriate.* San Francisco: Jossey-Bass.

> This sequel to Ernest Boyer's *Scholarship Reconsidered* provides a framework of six standards for evaluating the range of scholarly work that faculty undertake — be it basic research, applied work, or teaching. The six stan-

dards are clear goals, adequate preparation, appropriate methods, significant results, effective presentation, and reflective critique. As noted by both Mary Huber, in her "Why Now?" chapter, and by Daniel Bernstein, in his chapter on student learning, this framework is highly congruent with the model of the course portfolio set forth here in this volume.

Keig, Larry, and Michael D. Waggoner. 1994. *Collaborative Peer Review: The Role of Faculty in Improving College Teaching.* ASHE-ERIC Higher Education Reports, no. 2. Washington, DC: The George Washington University, School of Education and Human Development.
Only limited attention to portfolios, but powerful in its emphasis on the need for faculty to take active roles, as scholarly peers, in documenting and improving their individual and collective practice.

Palmer, Parker. November/December 1993. "Good Talk About Good Teaching: Improving Teaching Through Conversation and Community." *Change* 25 (6): 8-13.
Diagnoses "some of the deepest dissatisfactions in academic life" as products of the privatization of teaching (a condition the course portfolio seeks to relieve). Palmer proposes leadership strategies, topics, and ground rules for "creating a community of discourse about teaching and learning."

Quinlan, Kathleen, and Daniel J. Bernstein, eds. 1996. *Innovative Higher Education* 20 (4).
In this special issue of *IHE,* Quinlan and Bernstein pull together nine essays on the poor review of teaching, drawing primarily on the experience of faculty in AAHE's Peer Review of Teaching project. Especially useful is the focus, in any number of essays, on the relationship between "formative" (improvement-oriented) and "summative" (decision-making) uses of peer review, be it through portfolios or other strategies.

Shulman, Lee S. 1988. "Teaching Alone, Learning Together: Needed Agendas for the New Reforms." In *Schooling for Tomorrow: Directing Reform to Issues That Count,* edited by T.J. Sergiovanni and J.H. Moore, pp. 166-87. Boston: Allyn and Bacon.
Teaching is largely learned from experience, but "how does teaching become learning for the teacher?" This is of course a central question behind the course portfolio. Shulman examines what is required to learn from experience, including "the assistance of colleagues who can help us observe or monitor our own teaching behavior."

———. November/December 1993. "Teaching as Community Property: Putting an End to Pedagogical Solitude." *Change* 25 (6): 6-7.
This much-quoted, much-circulated essay stems from Shulman's "Displaying Teaching to a Community of Peers" plenary session address at the AAHE Conference on Faculty Roles & Rewards in San Antonio in January 1993. [An audiotape of that speech (#93CFRR-17) can be purchased from

the Mobiltape Company; call 1-800/369-5718.] Shulman's opening chapter here in this volume is in many ways the elaboration of that 1993 piece.

Weimer, Maryellen. November/December 1993. "The Disciplinary Journals on Pedagogy." *Change* 25 (6): 44-51.

One of the questions asked by faculty developing course portfolios is how to make them more broadly available. Websites (see section below) offer one possibility, but what of the more traditional discipline-based teaching journals? To what extent are they — or might they be — outlets for an emerging scholarship of teaching and learning? Weimer comments in depth on three of the more well-established such journals *(Journal of Marketing Education, Teaching of Psychology,* and *Journal of College Science Teaching).* But she also looks at the character of our published discourse about pedagogy more generally, calling for less imitation of traditional social science and more attention to alternative but rigorous forms and genres for representing what teachers know and do. The article ends with a thoughtful set of recommendations, which speak not only to the editors of these journals but to faculty wishing to direct their scholarship in this direction.

Web Resources

American Association for Higher Education (AAHE)
http://www.aahe.org

This site offers resources related to AAHE and its efforts: AAHE publications, upcoming conferences, descriptions of ongoing AAHE projects, and online versions of the *AAHE Bulletin,* among other items. Of particular use to those interested in course portfolios and the scholarship of teaching and learning is the "Teaching Initiatives" section (click on "Projects and Lines of Work" then "The Peer Review Project"), which includes numerous materials (exercises, detailed meeting agendas, links to campus reports and resources) from AAHE's project on the peer review of teaching.

Bass, Randy
http://www.georgetown.edu/bassr/portfolio/amlit/

This site provides the full hypertext portfolio described by Bass in case study 9 here in this volume.

Carnegie Foundation for the Advancement of Teaching
http://www.carnegie foundation.org

Among Carnegie's many past and present efforts to bring greater attention to the profession of teaching is a new five-year, $6 million partnership with the Pew Charitable Trusts aimed at "Fostering a Scholarship of Teaching and Learning." For an overview of that project — in which course portfolios will play an important role — click on "Carnegie Academy for the Scholarship of Teaching and Learning" on the second page of the statement from president Lee S. Shulman.

Crossroads Research Project

http://www.georgetown.edu/crossroads/conversations/

Crossroads is, as this site tells us, "a faculty study project on using technology to teach all areas of culture and history related to interdisciplinary American Studies." This site provides a forum for faculty to share and interact around case studies and examples of "ways to gauge student encounters with technology-enhanced pedagogies and practices" and discuss the implications of technology in teaching. In their complexity and "situatedness" case studies can be seen as cousins to course portfolios. Crossroads is directed by Randy Bass.

Cutler, William W., III

http://www.chnm.gmu.edu/aha

This site provides the full portfolio discussed in Cutler's case study 1 here in this volume. Click on "Teaching Concerns," then "AHA/AAHE Teaching Portfolios." The resulting section is the product of a collaboration between the American Historical Association (AHA) and AAHE's Peer Review of Teaching project, which resulted in a "history course portfolio working group" that operated in parallel with the multidisciplinary AAHE Course Portfolio Working Group.

Epiphany Project

http://www.urich.edu/~writing/websites.html

The Epiphany Project offers guidelines, resources, and examples to K-12 and postsecondary teachers hoping to use the Web in the classroom and to display their own work. This site is well organized and easily navigated.

Heath Anthology of American Literature

http://www.hmco.com/college/english/heath/index.html

This site is an online companion to the *Heath Anthology*, 3rd ed., edited by Paul Lauter. Of particular interest to those interested in course portfolios is the section "Hypertext Syllabus Builder," a feature designed and edited by Randy Bass, which includes accounts by faculty across the country of the rationale, conduct, and impact of their American literature courses.

National Board for Professional Teaching Standards

http://www.nbpts.org/nbpts/seeking/portfolio.html

The National Board for Professional Teaching Standards (NBPTS) is an independent, nonprofit organization aiming to establish "high and rigorous standards for what accomplished teachers should know and be able to do." Teachers who meet its standards can apply for National Board certification. This section of the NBPTS website provides guidelines for teachers who are developing a portfolio to submit as part of that application process. Also included are sample exercises from portfolios. The context is K-12, but the site is packed with information that could be helpful to higher education audiences.

Nottingham Trent University
http://celt.ntu.ac.uk/se/
   This site documents Nottingham's campus-wide Peer Review and Exchange
   of Teaching Excellence project and offers examples of case studies and portfolios written to document teaching. Related resources, including observation forms and evaluation strategies, are also provided.

University of Wisconsin-Madison, College of Engineering, Teaching Assistant
Fellows
http://www.cae.wisc.edu/~tafellow
   TAs in the college recently proposed and pioneered the writing of course
   portfolios as a method for learning from and building on teaching practice
   from semester to semester. For more about the effort, see the box in chapter
   6 here in this volume. For a look at the program's handbook for creating
   course portfolios, click on "Previous TA Fellows and Their Projects," then
   "Course Portfolio Development." You will need Adobe Acrobat Reader to
   view the handbook file; you can download the reader by clicking on "Get
   Acrobat Reader" and following the instructions.

Appendix

About the AAHE Teaching Initiatives

A program of the American Association for Higher Education, the AAHE Teaching Initiatives explore ways to develop campus cultures in which teaching contributes to student learning and engages the intellectual commitment of faculty. In this environment, teaching and learning are subjects of serious inquiry, discussion, and debate among faculty and others committed to educational improvement. Contributing to the development of a community of scholars who study and share findings about effective teaching and learning is the goal of the AAHE Teaching Initiatives.

The Carnegie Teaching Academy Campus Program

The Carnegie Teaching Academy Campus Program is being conducted by AAHE for the Carnegie Foundation for the Advancement of Teaching, with support from the Pew Charitable Trusts. The Campus Program is one part of the Foundation's larger, three-part Carnegie Teaching Academy. (For more about the Foundation, see **About the Carnegie Foundation for the Advancement of Teaching** below.)

The Campus Program is for institutions in all sectors prepared to make a public commitment to new models of teaching as scholarly work. The Program consists of three levels of participation. In the first level, Campus Conversations, campuses are invited to begin a two-part process of campus conversation, stocktaking, and planning, designed to set significant work in motion. In Part One of Campus Conversations, campuses examine a draft definition of "the scholarship of teaching" and identify supports and barriers to the scholarship of teaching and learning. In Part Two of Campus Conversations, campuses initiate a Campus Inquiry Group(s) to study and act on a teaching issue central to their campus.

After completing the Campus Conversations process, some of the campuses may be ready to move to a further stage of work — participation in a community of campuses. Campuses that have met the goals of the Campus Conversations process will be selected by the Campus Program for an opportunity to meet together, engage in collaborative activities, and report in multiple ways on outcomes of their campus activity.

In the Program's fourth year, institutions will be selected based on their participation in level one and level two of the Program to move to the final level of participation — more formal affiliation with the Carnegie Teaching Academy. These "affiliate" campuses will be eligible for small grants, consultancies, and national recognition.

Peer Collaboration and Review of Teaching

AAHE's recently concluded Peer Review of Teaching project developed new strategies through which faculty can make their work as teachers available to their scholarly peers for improvement-oriented exchange and for critique and review. The Teaching Academy Campus Program (above) extends and amplifies the work of many campuses from that peer review project. Active campuses have integrated new strategies of peer collaboration and review into regular practice and policy. New developments also have been advanced through partnerships with disciplinary and professional societies whose faculty members have been active in AAHE's peer review project.

Materials from and about the peer review project are available in the AAHE publications *Making Teaching Community Property: A Menu for Peer Collaboration and Peer Review* and *From Idea to Prototype: The Peer Review of Teaching (A Project Workbook)*. An additional place to look for information about the peer review project is the Teaching Initiatives page on AAHE's website.

Any campus interested in the peer review project's outcomes is invited to send for copies of its free brochure "Peer Collaboration and Review of Teaching." Send your request via email to aaheti@aahe.org; indicate the number of copies you need.

More Publications

Additional publications of the Teaching Initiatives contribute to the knowledge base about effective teaching and scholarship of teaching. These include *The Teaching Portfolio: Capturing the Scholarship in Teaching* and *Using Cases to Improve College Teaching: A Guide to More Reflective Practice*. To place an order or to request a catalog of all AAHE publications, contact AAHE Publications (202/293-6440 x11) or visit AAHE's website (www.aahe.org).

For More Information

To discuss the AAHE Teaching Initiatives or the Campus Program, contact Barbara Cambridge (x29), director, AAHE Teaching Initiatives, bcambridge@aahe.org. To inquire about Campus Program procedures, contact Teresa E. Antonucci (x34), program manager, AAHE Teaching Initiatives, tantonucci@aahe.org.

What Is AAHE?

The American Association for Higher Education (AAHE) is the individual membership organization that promotes the changes higher education must make to ensure its effectiveness in a complex, interconnected world. The association equips individuals and institutions committed to such changes with the knowledge they need to bring those changes about. For information about becoming an AAHE member, call the Membership Department at 202/293-6440 x27 or send email to pwaldron@aahe.org.

About the Carnegie Foundation for the Advancement of Teaching

The Carnegie Foundation for the Advancement of Teaching, founded in 1905 by Andrew Carnegie and incorporated in 1906 by an Act of Congress, is an independent institution devoted to strengthening teaching and learning in

America's colleges and schools. As expressed in its founding charter, the Foundation's mission is "to do and perform all things necessary to encourage, uphold, and dignify the profession of teaching."

Carnegie Teaching Academy

Among current projects of the Foundation is the Carnegie Teaching Academy, directed by Pat Hutchings. An ambitious multi-year project, which builds on developments with course portfolios featured in this volume, the Academy seeks to develop and shape a scholarship of teaching and learning that will (1) foster significant, long-lasting learning for all students, (2) enhance the practice and profession of teaching, and (3) bring to the faculty's work as teachers the recognition and stature afforded to other forms of scholarly work in higher education. Toward these ends, the Academy integrates work on three fronts:

The Pew Scholars Program brings together diverse faculty, 122 of them over the five years of the project, committed to investigating and documenting significant issues and challenges in the teaching of their fields. Each Scholar undertakes a project intended to contribute to a body of knowledge and practice in the teaching of his or her field. The Pew Scholars Program is not an award for teaching excellence; nor is it a teaching-improvement workshop. Its purpose is to create a community of scholars whose work will advance the profession of teaching and deepen the learning of students.

The Campus Program is designed to assist campuses in all sectors of higher education that are prepared to make a public commitment to develop models of teaching as scholarly work. As noted in **About the AAHE Teaching Initiatives** above, AAHE coordinates this aspect of the larger Carnegie project.

Work with the scholarly societies aims to promote teaching as scholarly activity within the national and international communities to which faculty belong as scholars in their fields.

For More Information

To learn more about the Carnegie Teaching Academy and other projects of the Carnegie Foundation, visit its website (www.carnegiefoundation.org). To add your name to the Carnegie Teaching Academy mailing list, contact Jacki Calvert, administrative assistant, The Carnegie Foundation for the Advancement of Teaching, 650/566-5139, calvert@carnegiefoundation.org.